C000149431

AMONG THE BOOKS in Wesley's library was *The Country Parson's Advice to His Parishioners*. It had made a deep impression on his mind at Oxford, and the little volume was highly prized and widely distributed by the members of the Holy Club. Its well-known suggestion as to the form of 'societies' had been accepted by many earnest men, and a striking example of the wisdom of the suggestion had been furnished by the founding of the 'Religious Societies', whose character and work we have described. The formation of Societies became one of Wesley's fixed ideas; he was not committed to the precise form they should assume, but he was convinced that, apart from the ordinary public services of the Church, it was expedient that opportunities should be provided for the more serious parishioners to assemble in private and informal meetings in which they might pray, sing, search the Scriptures, and help each other by religious conversation.

JOHN SIMON, in *John Wesley and the Religious Societies*

From prisoners to scholars, this classic guide was used by John and Charles Wesley for individuals seeking personal holiness, in small group study, and in the deepening of Christian life for English evangelicals at the Holy Club of Oxford.

THE COUNTRY-PARSON'S

ADVICE

—— TO HIS ——

Parishioners

A Serious Exhortation
To a Religious and Virtuous Life

ANONYMOUS

Last published in 1680.
Edited, revised and updated by
GEORGE BYRON KOCH

**MONARCH
BOOKS**

Copyright © George Byron Koch 1998

The right of George Byron Koch to be identified
as the editor of this work has been asserted by him in
accordance with Copyright, Designs
and Patents Act 1988

First published by Monarch Books 1998

ISBN 1 85424 407 8

All rights reserved.
No part of this publication may be reproduced or
transmitted in any form or by any means, electronic
or mechanical, including photocopy, recording or any information
storage and retrieval system, without permission in writing
from Monarch Books in association with Angus Hudson Ltd,
Concorde House, Grenville Place, Mill Hill, London NW7 3SA.

Editorial Office: Monarch Books,
Broadway House, The Broadway, Crowborough,
East Sussex TN6 1HQ.

Scripture quotations in this book are taken from the
Authorised Version of the Bible.

British Library Cataloguing in Publication Data
A catalogue record for this book is available
from The British Library.

Designed and produced for Angus Hudson Ltd by
Gazelle Creative Productions,
Concorde House, Grenville Place,
Mill Hill, London NW7 3SA.

C ONTENTS

PART 1 – *An Argument for Living A Holy Life*

PART 2 – *General Directions on How to Live a Holy and Christian Life*

ABOUT THE EDITOR

G EORGE BYRON KOCH (pronounced 'coke') is an evangelical Christian and Pastor of the Church of the Resurrection, an Episcopal church in West Chicago, Illinois. He is a widely published author on religion and other subjects. His writings have appeared in *Christianity Today*, the *Wall Street Journal*, the *University Bookman*, *Across the Board* (Conference Board Magazine) and the *Spiritual Counterfeits Project Journal* among others. He is also the author of a best-selling book on databases, titled *Oracle – the Complete Reference* (Osborne-McGraw/Hill, 1990-1998). He lives with his wife Victoria, and two boys, George and Isaiah, in Wheaton, Illinois.

ILLUSTRATED BY
NUMEROUS ENGRAVINGS ON WOOD FROM
DRAWINGS BY BIRKET FOSTER
AND JOHN GILBERT

FIRST PUBLISHED 1857
ADAM AND CHARLES BLACK
EDINBURGH.

ACKNOWLEDGEMENTS

M Y HEARTFELT THANKS go to John Todd, my faithful research assistant, for his labours in transcribing the original text of this book, and then completing the several revisions of it as I brought it into readable form in modern English. His good humour and ready willingness to help are deeply appreciated.

'Jesus said unto him, If thou wilt be perfect, go
and sell that thou hast, and give to the poor, and thou
shalt have treasure in heaven: and come
and follow me.'

INTRODUCTION TO THE NEW EDITION

 N 1680, IN THE REIGN OF CHARLES 2, an anonymous book entitled *The Country Parson's Advice to His Parishioners* was published in England. This was just two years after the formation in London, by Dr Horneck and the Rev. Smithies, of what came to be called the 'London Religious Societies'. These were a group of societies throughout London where young men met to 'edify one another' in their Christian faith. It is likely that the book was written by someone familiar with the societies, quite possibly a member or one of the founders. The 'small groups' or 'house churches' which have become so much a part of many vital churches today are based on the same approach to Christian fellowship and accountability.

Horneck produced rules for the societies' meetings. A sampling of them is reprinted here to give a sense of what the meetings were about:

1. All that enter the Society shall resolve upon a holy and serious life.

2. No person shall be admitted...until...first confirmed by the bishop, and solemnly taken upon himself his baptismal vow.

3. They shall choose a minister of the Church of England to direct them.

4. They shall not be allowed, in their meetings, to discourse of any controverted point of divinity.

5. Neither shall they discourse of the government of Church or State.

9. After all is done, if there be time left, they may discourse with each other about their spiritual concerns; but this shall not be a standing exercise which any shall be obliged to attend unto.

18. The following rules are more especially recommended to the members of this society, viz. To love one another. When reviled, not to revile again. To speak evil of no man. To wrong no man. To pray, if possible, seven times a day. To keep close to the Church of England. To transact all things peaceably and gently. To be helpful to each other. To use themselves to holy thoughts in their coming in and going out. To examine themselves every night. To give every one their due. To obey superiors, both spiritual and temporal.

Horneck was a genuine evangelical long before the evangelical revival of the eighteenth century. He spoke of the need for the 'new birth', and declared regularly the need for a 'real holiness of heart and life'. He preached to King William and Queen Mary, in November 1689, on 'The Nature of true Christian Righteousness', and emphasised 'consistent and holy living'. He also emphasised the need for true charity and spreading the gospel. The renowned Society for Promoting Christian Knowledge (SPCK), still a major Christian publisher and missionary society, is one of the direct products of the societies which he helped found. Bishop Overton, in his *Life in the English Church*, quotes Samuel Wesley, father of John and Charles, in both a sermon (1698) preached to one of the religious societies, and a letter (1699), to show Samuel Wesley's warm favour toward these groups.

Over the years these societies grew in number and vigour. Shortly after the turn of the eighteenth century, Dr Josiah Woodward wrote *Account of the Rise and Progress of the Religious Societies of London, &c.* (fourth edition dated 1712). Most of what we know of these societies comes from Woodward's book, and the book itself began a rapid multiplication of the societies in England, Germany and throughout the continent. The book contained not simply history, but the rules and patterns of conduct for the societies, allowing them easily to be modelled elsewhere. There are many parallels with the spread of small groups throughout the Christian world today.

Several interesting features of the meetings reveal the roots of the eventual Methodist breakaway at the end of the eighteenth century, and even evangelical practice up to the present era. Woodward assumed that the societies were in relationship with the Church of England, and preferred that each society have an ordained Church of England minister as its director, but the societies multiplied so rapidly that this became impractical. The rule was relaxed so that, in the absence of a minister, an order of service, based on the Church of England liturgy, could be used and led by a layman (recall that Horneck, earlier, had *required* a minister in rule 3). In the lay-led service, the word 'steward' was substituted for 'minister' in the liturgy, and each verse read was followed by a long pause to allow any one in the congregation to comment seriously on it. Members were also encouraged to share their spiritual experiences with one another (in contrast to Horneck's rule 9), and fervent singing was the norm: 'Let us, therefore, now strain up our affections to the highest pitch, and so sing the praises of God in heart and spirit, that angels and saints may join with us now, and we with them for evermore.' Today, we would refer to this layman as a 'lay pastor', the sharing of spiritual experiences as 'testimony', and fervent singing – unheard of and considered unseeming before the advent of these evangelicals – as 'praise and worship'.

THE WESLEYS

In November 1729, John and Charles Wesley and two others, William Morgan and Robert Kirkham, began meeting regularly at Oxford to study the Greek New Testament and Latin and

Greek classics. In the summer of 1730, Morgan visited a prison, and returned convinced of the need to bring the gospel inside the prison walls. At his suggestion, the Wesleys began regular visitations to the prisoners, preaching, teaching and taking care of their families. Books were read to the prisoners, among them *The Country Parson's Advice to his Parishioners*, followed by conversation and fellowship. Some thirty years later, John Wesley wrote of this book,

> I met with a book written in King William's time [actually Charles 2] called *The Country Parson's Advice to His Parishioners*. There I read these words: 'If Good men of the Church will unite together in the several parts of the kingdom, disposing themselves into friendly societies, and engaging each other…it will be the most effectual means for restoring our decaying Christianity to its primitive life and vigour, and the supporting of our tottering and sinking Church.' (See page 90.)

This sage advice from this small book and its anonymous author, is as apt today as it was when written, and the church in many parts of the globe – especially in the 'civilised' world – is certainly 'tottering and sinking'.

John Simon, in *John Wesley and the Religious Societies* (Epworth Press: London, 1921), says:

> Among the books in Wesley's library was *The Country Parson's Advice to His Parishioners*. It had made a deep impression on his mind at Oxford, and the little volume was highly prized and widely distributed by the members of the Holy Club. Its well-known suggestion as to the form of 'societies' had been accepted by many earnest men, and a striking example of the wisdom of the suggestion had been furnished by the founding of the 'Religious Societies', whose character and work we have described. The formation of Societies became one of Wesley's fixed ideas; he was not

committed to the precise form they should assume, but he was convinced that, apart from the ordinary public services of the Church, it was expedient that opportunities should be provided for the more serious parishioners to assemble in private and informal meetings in which they might pray, sing, search the Scriptures, and help each other by religious conversation. He lost no time in forming such a Society in Savannah. He tells us in his Journal, that it began in April, 1736.

The small group at Oxford grew somewhat, and was widely known there and ridiculed for its efforts at personal holiness and its work with the poor and imprisoned. It was nicknamed the 'Holy Club' by its critics, and John Wesley, with an eye for irony, adopted the name for the group. The group 'carefully read and industriously distributed' the 'Country Parson's' book, modelling their own activities, and their focus on personal holiness, on the methods given in the text. Among other suggestions given in the book is the complete application of personal fortune to God's work. This is precisely what the English evangelicals did during the eighteenth century. Typical were those known later as the 'Clapham Sect', including William Wilberforce, John Venn, Zachary Macaulay, Lord Teignmouth, Henry Thorton, Granville Sharp and Hannah More, who gave unsparingly of their time and wealth to charitable work. Many of them had given away virtually all they owned by the time of their deaths. In addition to their lengthy opposition to slavery, much of their money and attention was focused on local missions for the poor, the blind, the imprisoned, foundlings, widows, sailors, Germans, Russians, Spaniards, and many more. The list of their charitable Christian works is lengthy and nearly unbelievable to modern sensibilities.

Whether this great willingness to give everything for the gospel can be traced to the influence of this book we can only speculate. Consider this little vignette about George Whitefield, from Gordon Rupp's book *Religion in England* (Clarendon Press: Oxford, 1986):

> George Whitefield was a latecomer [to the Holy Club] and very much the ugly duckling. One morning in September 1732 Charles Wesley got a message, passed on by an old apple woman, and invited the sender to breakfast. He recognized him as one he had seen mooching about Oxford by himself, but the thin young man with a cast in his eye, woollen gloves, patched gown, was not pre-possessing. Rightly suspecting fear of ridicule had kept him away, he lent him Francke's *Nicodemus, the Fear of Man* and the much praised *Country Parson's Advice to his Parishioners*, and promised to keep an eye on him. (p. 339)

Clearly, it seeded and inspired the Wesleys and the Holy Club, as well as many others whom they taught, with a vigour and passion for God which was virtually unknown in the church of their day, as it is in ours.

We see in the remarkable eighteenth century the roots of much modern evangelical practice, as well as the reawakening of religious societies, clearly inspired and undergirded by this notable book, *The Country Parson's Advice to His Parishioners*. Yet no evidence can be found that this book was ever reprinted after its first edition in 1680. This new edition is therefore the only opportunity most of the Christian community will have to see what it was that so inspired the Wesleys and the evangelicals of their time. It is extraordinarily challenging and difficult, in that it issues a call to repentance and obedience that most modern Christians – even those we would judge as serious and mature – would regard as impossible to fulfil.

Even so, it provides insights into our conduct, and the depth and nature of our faith, that can't but change the manner in which we respond to our Lord's calls to perfection, in particular in Matthew 19:21 – 'Jesus said unto him, "If thou wilt be perfect, go and sell that thou hast, and give to the poor, and thou shalt have treasure in heaven: and come and follow me."'

Great Christians, including John and Charles Wesley – who have so formed evangelical thought and community even to this day – found this book of fundamental and enduring value. They used it and taught from it – prisoners and scholars alike. It is only simple wisdom that tells us to study and heed it well.

NOTES ON THIS EDITION

FIRST CAME ACROSS a reference to this book during research I was doing on evangelicals in the Anglican and Episcopal Church. Early attempts to locate a copy of it proved fruitless, and only after several worldwide book searches was a microfilmed copy found. It was a fascinating search, and its difficulty proved to make it only that much more intriguing. Yet when it was – at last! – located and read, it became apparent that what was surely clear and straightforward prose in 1680 was difficult and often obscure for the modern reader. To be of the same value as it was to the evangelicals of the eighteenth century, it would need to be put into more modern prose.

The task of updating the text of a book written three hundred years ago is considerable, and although not nearly so difficult, it provides fresh appreciation for those scholars engaged in translating the Bible from Hebrew or Greek into English. The English language, grammar and writing styles of 1680 differ in many ways from those of the late twentieth century, and although it is possible to read most sentences of that time and deduce their meaning, the effort can prove very tedious.

In order to maximise the benefit of this wonderful text, and make it accessible to as wide an audience as possible, certain updates were made to the language, grammar and style – all with a careful eye to preserve the original author's tone and message. For example, commas and semicolons were used in the original at a rate, and with rules of placement, which to today's reader would seem almost absurd, and render the text often impenetrable. These were reduced, and occasionally moved, to conform to modern standards of punctuation. Many sentences of that day were extremely long, and contained numerous clauses and subclauses which referred back to distant parts of the same sentence. These were broken up into simpler sentences without loss of meaning, but with considerable gain in clarity.

In addition, some words and idioms have either vanished from the language or changed meaning so substantially that they would also render the text inaccessible or cause us to misconstrue its intent. An example of this is the word 'discover', which in 1680 was used to mean 'admit', as in 'I must discover my sins to my brothers.' That is, not that I was to find my sins for the first time, but that I was to *un*-cover them to others.

A second example is found in some instances in the text of the more archaic uses of 'brother' and 'men' which no longer retain the inclusive connotation of their day for the average modern reader. These are not changed everywhere, nor are pronouns such as 'he' and 'his' as they often would be today, but rather just in those instances when the older usage proved awkward or confusing.

Yet another example is the word 'conventing', which means to summon or convene, but which doesn't even appear in many modern dictionaries – or, when its verb root 'convent' does appear, it is labelled 'obscure'. This and all such archaic words are replaced by a modern word or idiom which conveys the essential meaning that the original word held in 1680.

Finally, there was an extremely small amount of material which reflected local religious controversies underway in England at the time, and which was simply superfluous, especially for the modern reader. This has been removed because it was confusing and misdirecting.

Apart from these essential updates, *The Country Parson's Advice to His Parishioners* is as intact as the English evangelicals, and in particular the Wesleys and the Holy Club, knew it and used it in their ministry. May it again prove valuable to the community of believers.

George Byron Koch, Wheaton, Illinois, September 1996

Right: Facsimile of the original title page published in 1680.

THE

COUNTRY-PARSON'S

ADVICE

TO HIS

Parishioners.

In Two Parts.

I. Containing a Plain and Serious Exhortation to a Religious and Virtuous Life.

II. General Directions how to Live accordingly.

LONDON,

Printed for *Benj. Tooke*, at the *Ship* in St. *Paul's* Church-yard, 1 6 8 o.

INTRODUCTION

I DESIGN, THROUGH GOD'S GRACE, to give you the best assistance I can in a religious and virtuous life; to direct you how to live to God's glory, and to attain that perfect and happy estate which God has made you capable of, and which your Saviour desires to bring you to, by that holy religion which you profess. But before you accept my assistance and direction, it may be that you would desire to know whether there is any reason why you should apply yourself to live such a life, and whether you may not as prudently let it alone, and live as most of your neighbours do.

Therefore I desire that you would do me and yourself the kindness, seriously to consider the following things.

PART 1

An Argument for Living A Holy Life

Therefore I must beseech you to consider
for what end God gave you your being.

CHAPTER
1
==

CONTAINING THE FIRST ARGUMENT TO A HOLY LIFE, THAT
BEING GOD'S CREATURES WE OUGHT TO BE SUBJECT TO
GOD, AS ALL OTHER CREATURES ARE, TO OBSERVE THE
LAWS OF OUR CREATION, AND TO CONSULT THE HONOUR
AND DIGNITY OF OUR NATURES.

 OREASMUCH AS YOU KNOW that you are God's creature, and received being and life from him, and subsist altogether in him, you must necessarily acknowledge that you are and ought to be at his disposal, and to live and act according to his intention, and the end for which you were made. As you are God's creature, and have no other being than what you have received from him, also you can have no power nor end, but what he gives and prescribes to you. This is a law which all the creatures of God are subject to, and you see that all the inferior creatures act according to it: they employ themselves according to the capacity of their being, in that for which God created them, and tend directly to the end for which they were created and ordained. Therefore you cannot but know that you ought to do likewise, and that for whatever end you were created, you are constantly to intend and do the same in your whole life.

Could you give life and being to any thing, you would justly expect the same from it. Therefore I must beseech you to consider for what end God gave you your being. Now you are aware that you have an excellent being and that the other creatures, which you see in the world, are much inferior to you.

31

You have understanding, and by that the knowledge of things which other creatures have not and cannot have of things spiritual and immaterial. You have a free will to choose or refuse, according to the direction of your understanding, without coercion or compulsion; whereas they act necessarily, and without any such liberties. You have desires implanted in your soul after things which they have no apprehension of; and you are capable of some enjoyments which they are altogether incapable of. To what end, then, have you this excellent being bestowed upon you, and what is it that you are to aim at, to desire and endeavour toward, while you are in the world?

Can you think, when you consider your own faculties and capacities, that you were made merely to get a little money by burdening and caring, by toiling and sweating, by plotting and contriving?

A poor business surely for such an excellent creature! And you debase yourself extremely, and reproach your maker, if you imagine it. But you know that money is not a thing desirable for itself, but for its usefulness as it procures necessities, and things pleasing to appetites and desires. Therefore, you must enquire further, whether you were made only to eat and drink, and having made provision for the flesh, to fulfil the lusts thereof. I beseech you, tell me whether this will not sink you down into the condition of the beasts and birds, and reflect as injuriously upon your Maker. Certainly, they are as capable of such gratifications and satisfactions as you are, notwithstanding your excellent spirit and better capacities. They can feast as gustfully upon those provisions that God has made for them as you can, and sing as merrily. You do not clothe your workers in purple and fine linen to send them to the plough, nor bring up children in all the polite learning of the world on purpose to employ them in feeding hogs. And if you should see your neighbour act so foolishly, you would not fail to deride him for it. Will you dare to impute the like folly to the wise creator and governor of the world, and believe that he has given you an immortal spirit, to be employed only about the objects of sense, to the end that you may live like the beasts and perish?

Far be it from you. You are made certainly for a much better and nobler end than they were. The powers and capacities of your soul would lead you to the knowledge of it, even if God had given you no other means of knowing it. You are capable of knowing your creator, of contemplating his infinite perfections, of admiring and praising, and loving what you know. Though you live in the world, yet you can have your mind in heaven, and dwell with God by desire and love; and if you can feast your senses upon these material and perishing things, you can surely feast your spirit much more upon the never failing wisdom and goodness of the maker of all things. You know him to be the supreme good, and that every thing is good and happy only so far as it partakes of his goodness and felicity; and you know that there can be no other way to perfect happiness than to give up yourself wholly to him, to submit to his government and conduct, to do whatever he will have you to do, to suffer all that he will lay upon you. Have your eye always upon him, delight yourself in him, desire and hope more fully and perfectly to know him and enjoy him.

These things you know or may know, and you are capable of acting according to your knowledge: you can give yourself to God, you can submit yourself to him, you can serve him and obey him with a cheerful and active service, you can praise and magnify him, and rely upon him, and hope and long for a complete growth in him.

Behold then, what you were created to do, and observe how you are to employ yourself in the world. Here is your end, and this is your work, a work worthy of so excellent a creature: to serve God. Whatsoever you do, or endeavour to do, or spend your time in, that is contrary to this end, is but vanity and folly, is mere lost labour, and will bring forth no fruit but grief and sorrow, shame and confusion. For that is not the work that we came into the world to do. We were made in the image of God, not to live like beasts, no, nor to please ourselves in any way; but to serve and please and glorify God here, and to possess and enjoy him for ever hereafter. Judge then whether you have not reason to serve God with all your might in a holy and virtuous life.

CHAPTER
2
==

CONTAINING A SECOND ARGUMENT TO A HOLY LIFE,
FROM THOSE OBLIGATIONS WHICH OUR PROFESSION OF
CHRISTIANITY LAYS ON US.

F YOU PROFESS YOURSELF a Christian, I must ask you to consider seriously what that Christianity is which you profess, and what the profession of it requires you to do. To this purpose, I beseech you to reflect upon your baptism and to call to mind what was then transacted and done between God and your soul, or (which is all one) between God and the Church in your behalf. Now, in that holy ceremony you were dedicated to God the Father, Son and Holy Ghost; and, renouncing the world, the flesh and the devil, you promised obedience to all his commandments. God mercifully accepted your renunciation and dedication, and took you into his house and family – that family which Christ purchased with his blood, and which he governs by his Spirit, and for which he has prepared everlasting bliss and glory.

You were then taken off that rotten and corrupt vine of the first and earthly Adam, which brings forth fruit only to death and destruction, and grafted into the living vine of the second and spiritual Adam, which yields fruit to everlasting glory and happiness. You renounced that principle of sin and death, which you derived from your first parents, and whatever encourages it. Giving up yourself to God you were received by him and given to his son Jesus Christ, who took possession of you by his Spirit, which becomes new life in you. That all this is done in baptism – not in ceremony and by representation only; but in deed and in real effect. This is plain enough in the Scriptures. You may look into the following places for your satisfaction:

Our blessed Saviour tells us, in John 15:5 – *'I am the Vine, and you are the branches; he that abides in me and I in him, brings forth much fruit.'*

Now, this abiding in him presupposes our ingrafting into him: and this was done in our baptism. For then, as the Apostle St Paul tells us in First Corinthians 12:13, *'We are baptised by one spirit into one body.'* And that body is *'the body of Christ'* as you will see in verse 27 of the same chapter.

In Galatians 3:27 we are said in baptism to *'put on Christ.'*

In Romans 6:5 we are said *'to be united together* (namely by baptism) *in the likeness of Christ's death'*, and by this the same Apostle tells us, in Titus 3:5, that we are saved: *'According to his mercy he saved us, by the washing of regeneration, and renewing of the Holy Ghost.'*

We cannot (ordinarily) be saved without this washing and renewing. Our blessed Saviour told Nicodemus (John 3:5): *'Except a man be regenerated of water, and the Spirit, he cannot enter into the Kingdom of God.'*

These places of Scripture being understood in that sense, which the first and best Christians took them in, taught us all that which I said before concerning baptism. The Church teaches us the same, both in the office of baptism and the catechism, telling us that in baptism *'we are regenerated, and made members of Christ, and inheritors of* (that is, we have a right thereby to inherit) *the Kingdom of Heaven.'*

You see then, dear friend, what you are as a Christian, and what you profess yourself to be: you are separated from the world, dedicated and consecrated to God, united to Christ Jesus, and in him and by him a child of God, and an heir of everlasting life. You are not your own, therefore, but God's. And

We cannot (ordinarily) be saved without
this washing and renewing.

you are his, not only by creation, but by redemption and purchase, by your own act of voluntary resignation of your self to him, by covenant and promise, by a real incorporation into the body of Christ, and the participation of his Spirit.

This is an honourable and a happy estate, and it was a wonderful grace that such a worthless, rebellious creature should ever be admitted into it. And need I now to ask you, friend, what kind of life ought you to live? It is a rule in nature that such as a being is, such will the actions and operations of it be. Therefore it is necessary that your life and actions are agreeable to your being and state, as you are a Christian; and since the estate of a Christian is a holy and divine estate, it is necessary that your life and actions are holy and divine. Are you a member of Christ, ingrafted into his body and quickened by his Spirit? And ought you not to be conformed to Christ and to live the life of Christ? Are you a child of God and ought you not to be *'led by the spirit of God'* (Romans 8:14). And to *'be a follower or imitator of God'* (Ephesians 5:1) in love and purity? Are you not *'an heir of heaven'* (Romans 8:17)?

And ought not *your* conversation be in heaven? Ought not your thoughts and desires to be upon your 'inheritance'; and your heart and life to be such as may render you appropriate to be a partaker of it (Colossians 1:12)?

Would not you wonder to see the pleasant vine degenerate into a sorry thistle, and the fruitful olive into an unprofitable bramble? Isn't this what you do, if being a Christian you live like a heathen, if being in the Spirit you walk after the flesh, and mind the things of the flesh? Was it not a most dreadful curse that drove the great King Nebuchadnezzar out of his stately palace into the fields among the beasts, to eat grass like the oxen, in Daniel 4? And do you not make his curse to be your own choice when, being a child of God, an heir of the kingdom of heaven (which is more than to be emperor of the whole earth), you set your heart upon this dunghill world, and have no esteem or relish of heavenly things? Is this not what you choose if, with profane Esau, you sell your birthright for a bowl of stew, and despising your eternal inheritance, desire to have your portion only in this life?

The reason of all this is plain enough, and I hope will be readily acknowledged by you: however impossible it is you must confess that you are obliged to perform your promises, and to pay your vows unto the most high. Since you have given up yourself to God, you have not the least power over yourself, but ought to live altogether in him. If you have an ill opinion of your neighbour, and that justly, when he is not as good as his word to you, how can you but condemn yourself when you break your vows unto the Lord? When any profane thing has been offered to God, and consecrated by prayer and ceremonies, and set apart for holy and divine purposes, and you esteem it as separated from common use, then you call it sacrilege and profane to employ it in common ways. Are you then not yourself also guilty of the highest sacrilege when, being dedicated and consecrated to God by baptism, you withdraw yourself from him, and never employ yourself for him, nor refer yourself to him? The apostle tell us, *'That we are not our own, because we are bought with a price'* (that is, the blood of the Son of God) in 1 Corinthians 6:19,20).

And I add to it: we have given up ourselves to him that bought us. Therefore, there is the greatest reason that we should glorify him in our bodies, and our spirits, which are God's. It was the sayings of a devout man many years ago, *'That it had been better for us never to have been, than to dwell in ourselves and to our selves'*.

We shall find it too true one day if, forgetting our state and profession, and obligation as we are Christians, we do live to ourselves and not to God.

Then, consider whether there is not reason enough
why you should be careful to lead
a virtuous and holy life.

CHAPTER
3
≡

ONSIDER THAT THERE WILL COME a time when you
must give an exact account of your life and actions;
and it shall be known to all the world, how you
have demeaned yourself, both as a person and
Christian. Dear friend, do you believe the Scriptures? I know
you do, and you have the greatest reason in the world to do so.
Observe therefore what they tell you concerning that account
which you are to make. Then, consider whether there is not
reason enough why you should be careful to lead a virtuous and
holy life. It is a mighty encouragement indeed to us in doing
good that our Saviour is to be our judge; for he, who loved his
enemies so as to die for them, will never forget the good works
of those whom he *'calls his friends'* (John 15:14).

But lest any of us should be so unwise as to make this an
argument for a licentious and careless way of living, promising
ourselves much favour from him, and an easy account at the day
of judgement, he has told us frequently that he purposes to proceed severely with us, and to show no favour but what may consist with exact justice. And it well deserves our observation
that, although he was the mildest and most merciful person
alive, and expressed the greatest tenderness and love to sinful
men and women that ever was, so much so that his enemies cast
it as a reproach upon him, that he was a friend to publicans and
sinners; yet he never spoke of the day of judgement but with
great severity. Nor did he speak of himself, as the judge of the

world, but in such words as altogether exclude that fond partiality which wicked men expect from him at that day. Thus in one place he represents himself to be an austere and hard man, and tells us *that he expects to reap, where he did not sow, and to gather where he did not* winnow. That is, he will expect, and require from us (when he comes to judge us) an increase of those talents which he has entrusted us with; and if we have not improved them to his advantage, he will *'first take them away from us, and then cast us into a prison of darkness, where shall be weeping, and gnashing of teeth'* (Matthew 25:30).

And we may note there that it is with the *unprofitable servant*, the servant that brought him no increase, that he will deal so severely. Therefore, how rigorously may we believe he will deal with those that do misspend his talents, and make no use of them, but to his dishonour? In the same chapter we find him no less severe to five foolish virgins, whom he shuts for ever out of heaven, *'because they had no oil with their lamps, and were not ready exactly at the hour* (though it was midnight) *to meet the bridegroom'* (Matthew 25:12). In another place he condemns to everlasting misery, not only those who do not accept his invitation to his marriage feast, but *'those likewise that came to it without wedding garments'* (Matthew 22:12,13). And in the seventh chapter of the same Gospel he declares, *'That this shall be the portion of all the workers of iniquity, though they have called him Lord, and prophesied in his name, and cast out devils, and done many wonderful works.'*

That is, though they have professed themselves his disciples and servants and done some things which the world accounts great, for his honour, yet he will not own them. Though they make fair pleas for themselves, and beg his mercy and favour with the greatest earnestness and importunity, yet he will have no regard unto them, but banish them for ever from him.

All this, and much more than this, has our blessed Saviour

told us by way of parable. And he has nowhere encouraged us to hope for anything more easy and favourable, when he speaks plainly of it and without a parable. He has let us know in plain words that he will judge our works, nay, our very words also, and require an account not only of our filthy and ungodly speeches, *'but of our idle, our vain and unprofitable discourses likewise'* (Matthew 12:36). Even more, he has told us, *'that the very thoughts and purposes of our hearts shall be brought into judgement. The offending eye, the lustful, adulterous eye may cause the whole body to be cast into hell. And that a causeless anger entertained against our brother or sister, though it show itself neither by words, nor deeds, will bring us into danger of condemnation'* (Matthew 5:22b,23).

You will think these hard sayings, it may be; and yet there is somewhat more to be considered which may make you think them much harder. Might our judgement be in private, and our accounts be made between God and ourselves only, we might, notwithstanding all that which has been said, look upon it as tolerable. But, alas! We are told that it must be public (without any regard to our modesty) and before all the world, that *'the very secrets of our hearts shall be disclosed before men and angels, and the hidden things of darkness shall be brought to light'* (1 Corinthians 4:5) and *'all our counsels be made manifest'*.

And further, that this shall be at a time when (perhaps) we did not look for it, at midnight or at cocks-crowing; that we may be hurried away to Christ's judgement-seat before we can trim our lamps, or make ready our accounts, or think what course to take to approve ourselves to our judge and Lord. We may be eating and drinking, or buying and selling, or planting and building (as the people were in Noah's day when the flood came and swept them all away) and the Son of man shall be revealed from heaven, and we shall be taken as in a snare. We shall not be able to flee away from him, nor to stand before him, because we are not prepared and ready for him (see Luke

43

17:26-28). His coming, we are told, will be with so much majesty and glory, so many dreadful things shall go before it, and so much terror accompany it, that we shall be utterly confounded, and not able to lift up our heads, if clear and good consciences, and just and right accounts prepared and made ready before hand, do not give us some confidence and assurance before him:

'The heaven shall pass away with a great noise, and the elements shall melt with a fervent heat, and the earth and all the works that are therein shall be burnt up' (2 Peter 3:10), and then 'shall the Lord Jesus descend from heaven with a shout, with the voice of the archangel, and the trump of God' (1 Thessalonians 4:16) and all 'the nations and kindreds of the earth, and those that are in their graves shall hear his voice' (John 5:28) and behold his glory, 'the glory of the king of kings, and of the Lord of Lords, who treads the winepress of the fierceness and wrath of Almighty God' (Revelation 19:15,16).

What will you do in that day? And what shall I do who now ask you the question? How shall we be able to bear the sight of so great a majesty and glory? How shall we have the courage to appear before it? What dread, what horror will possess our souls? What confusion will cover our faces? How shall we tremble when we think of our trial before that impartial and dreadful bar? And how will our hearts sink within us when we are called to answer for ourselves?

What will a good conscience, do you think, be worth at that day? What would you then give for a pure and unspotted life, to present before the just judge of heaven and earth? What would you give for as great a number of good works as you have of sins and rebellions and provocations? Whatever you think of a good life now, believe it. You will then think well of it, and thrice happy shall you be, if your own heart condemns you not of wickedness and impiety. Whether it will do so or not, I am not able to tell you. But this I can assure you, that no tongue is

What would you then give for a pure and
unspotted life,
to present before the just judge
of heaven and earth?

able to express the amazement and consternation, the horror and anguish, the perplexity that shall possess and overwhelm you, if it condemns you.

You will not know what course to take, which way to look. To avoid the judgement will be impossible, and you will not be able to bear it. If you call for mercy you shall find none; if you desire death, your desire will not be granted, and if you call to the hills to cover you, they shall be deaf to you. All hope, all comfort shall utterly forsake you, and you must stand at the dreadful tribunal as a desperate and helpless wretch, till you hear that dreadful and irrevocable sentence, 'Depart from me you cursed into everlasting fire, prepared for the devil, and his angels.'

And now, tell me, I beseech you, what thoughts you have of a holy life? Is there any reason why you should be careful to lead such a life, or not?

Do you think that you can avoid this dreadful account we have spoken of? Or do you hope that an account made according to that careless and carnal way of living which we see most people live, will pass at that just tribunal, and be accepted as good? Can you have the face to make before God and all the world such a declaration as this? God gave me an excellent being, I acknowledge, and appointed me an excellent end, but I neither considered the one, nor thought upon the other. God made me capable to know him, and worship and serve him, and I was frequently told that the main business of my life was to do thus. But this I never intended nor designed, or if I did, it was but now and then, and when I had nothing else to do.

I cannot deny that I was capable of bringing my maker a great increase of glory, by the use and improvement of those excellent faculties he bestowed upon me; but the lusts and appetites of the flesh, and the pleasures of providing for and satisfying them, made me forget myself and the honour of him that made me.

I must acknowledge likewise, that it was not ordinary grace which called me to the knowledge of Christ, and that I thought myself partaker of no little honour and advantage by it. But whether my Christianity laid any other obligations upon me than the bearing the name of a Christian, I could never find time to consider, nor think it worth while to enquire. I thought better of myself, indeed, than of other men, for my being a Christian. But that I have lived better than they, that I have been more mindful of God and more profitable to men, I am not able to say.

I have talked much of heaven, but I ever loved the world before I loved it. Though I professed great love to Christ, yet my main business has always been to please myself. I know you will cry out upon this as most absurd and unreasonable, and conclude it impossible any person should find mercy at that great day, that can speak nothing better for himself. Yet I defy all our common careless Christians to make any better plea for themselves, or to give any better account of themselves and those talents that God has entrusted them with. Have you a child or employee, whom you have bestowed great cost upon, to fit him for doing for you some considerable and important service? And have you committed it to his care and charge, given him a competent time, and furnished him with all necessaries and requisites for the doing it? And that child or employee after his time expired returns to give you such an account as this? 'So much of my time I spent in eating and drinking, in revelling and rioting, in singing and dancing, in courting and sporting, about which all my thoughts and all my care were wholly taken up. As for the great business you commanded me to do, I never thought upon it, or at least not till it was too late. Then I had neither time nor other requisites remaining to effect it.'

Would not such a child or employee vex you to the heart?

47

And would not you think him worthy of the greatest shame and punishment? Remember that it will be your own case if, neglecting the great end of thy life and being, and the indispensable obligations of your most holy religion, you can only reckon at that great day your getting and spending of money for the satisfaction of your beastly lusts and appetites.

CHAPTER

4

CONTAINING A FOURTH ARGUMENT TO A HOLY LIFE, THE
CONSIDERATION OF THE FUTURE PUNISHMENTS OF THE
WICKED: THAT THEIR TORMENTS ARE EXTREME AND
INTOLERABLE, WITHOUT CEASING AND WITHOUT END.

CONSIDER THE PUNISHMENTS which almighty God has prepared for those unfaithful people, who will not be able to stand in that judgement, but must fall under the dreadful sentence of condemnation. And that you may know how great those punishments will be, you will do well to call to mind what punishments God has often inflicted upon the wicked in this world. I omit the effects of Adam's sin and disobedience, which the whole world still labours under, as also the fruits of our own sins, which perhaps we have more than once smarted for. Let it be remembered how God destroyed all mankind except eight persons, with a flood of water, for their sins (Genesis 7). How he overthrew five cities with fire and brimstone for their filthiness and impiety (Genesis 19). How he destroyed his own people, for whom he had wrought many wonders in the wilderness, when they would not obey his voice, *'causing twenty three thousand of them to fall in one day'* (1 Corinthians 10:8). How he gave commandment utterly to destroy the Amalekites, and not to spare their sucking children, for a sin committed by their fathers four hundred years before: and in a word, how he gave up his own once beloved people and their city and country, to the most lamentable ruin and desolation that ever was; and how their posterity scattered to this day over the face of the whole earth. *'His blood be upon us, and our children'* (Matthew 27:25).

These are great demonstrations of God's hatred against sin, and from these we learn that those punishments which are appointed for wicked men in another world must needs be very grievous, and will make them extremely miserable. For, as the Scriptures tell us, this is the time of God's patience, and forbearance and goodness towards sinners (Romans 2:4), and if in this time he shows so much severity, how severe may we believe he will be, when this time of his goodness is ended, and when the day of his wrath, as the Scripture calls it, is come; that day of justice without mercy, of vengeance without pity, of execution without further patience and forbearance: when all the wrath that wicked men have deserved, and have treasured up against themselves, shall fall upon their guilty souls, and God shall magnify his imperial justice in their torment and misery, as he will magnify his mercy and goodness in the glory and felicity of his faithful servants?

But we have yet a better way of learning how great the punishments of the damned shall be, and that is by considering what the Scriptures have told us in plain words concerning them. They are such punishments, our blessed Saviour tells us, *'as are prepared for the devil and his angels'* (Matthew 25:41). That is, for the very worst of beings, for the greatest rebels against heaven, and the most irreconcilable adversaries to all manner of goodness. Therefore, we may be sure that they are at least as great as we can imagine them to be, even more great since an almighty God makes them. They are punishments by fire, as he also tells us, which is the most raging, the most devouring and tormenting thing we know in the world: and that fire is represented to be such as our nature most abhors, and must be most insufferable, namely, *'a fire with brimstone'* (sulphur), the stench of which is as intolerable as the heat, and which suffocates as well as consumes (Revelation 21:8). Of this fire, we are told likewise, *'there is a bottomless lake or pit'* (Revelation 20:3). Into it there shall never enter the least light, the very *'blackness of darkness'*, as St Jude's expressions are (Jude 1:13), lying upon it for ever. In this lake, we are told, the damned shall be shut in as prisoners, *'bound hand and foot'* (Matthew 22:13). They will be without possibility of escaping, or so much as moving from one place to another for the gaining of the least ease; and in this prison we are told the torments will be such as will cause *'weeping and wailing and gnashing of teeth'*, nay, yellings and howlings, and shriekings *'like the shrieking of the children frying in the fire in the Valley of Hinnom'* (2 Kings 23:10).

This is a punishment which the word used by our blessed Saviour for hell, Gehenna (Matthew 5:29,30) implies. And these torments and wailings and heart-breaking cries shall continue, not for a month, or a year, or an age, but for ever and ever. *'The fire shall never be quenched'* (Mark 9:44). *'The smoke of their torment is ever to ascend'* (Revelation 14:10,11), *'and they shall find no rest night nor day'*. This is but a little of what the Scripture tells us of the punishments of the damned; but in this little there are so many dreadful things implied that he must be bold and hardened even to a wonder that is not frightened with them.

4.1 TORMENT SHALL BE GREAT

For it is plain that the punishments are such as will torment the whole person, body and soul, with all their faculties and powers, and that in the most extreme manner. There shall not be a member of the body, nor any faculty in the soul, but shall have its torment in one and the same instant, and that torment shall be so great that no words can express it, nor heart can conceive it. How can it be otherwise, do you think, in a lake of fire and brimstone? What member of the body will not be scorched? What sense will not be afflicted? What faculty will not be tormented?

The lascivious eyes will be plagued with darkness, and the ugly and fearful fight of devils and damned spirits. The nice smell will be plagued with the loathsome stench of brimstone, and all the most abominable filthiness. The delicate ears with the shrieks and howlings of tormenting, and tormented wretches. The dainty taste will be plagued with the most ravenous hunger and thirst, and all the sensible parts with burning and devouring fire. The imagination will have its torment by the apprehension of present pains, and of those that are to come. The memory by its remembrance of pleasures past and gone, and never to return again. The understanding by the consideration of the happiness lost, and the misery now come on. And if there be any other part which can be tormented, it shall have its torment with no more favour than the rest. What sad and dreadful things are these! And how unspeakably miserable must those be who must endure them! And yet this is not all; for it is certain in the second place...

4.2 THE TORMENTS WILL NOT CEASE

These torments shall always continue without the least intermission or decrease, and those that suffer them shall never find the least ease, nor help, nor comfort; no, not for one minute. This is no more than is implied in the places of Scripture before mentioned. The fire will be always burning, the smoke ever ascending, so that there shall be no rest day or night, and those that are bound hand and foot will not be able to escape or to resist, or strive against the torments, but must lie still and suffer all. Thus it was with the rich man, of whom our blessed Saviour tells us (Luke 16:24), that being in hell, tormented with the fire which shall not be quenched, he made this request to Abraham: *'Father Abraham have mercy on me, and send Lazarus, that he may dip the tip of his finger in water and cool my tongue, for I am tormented in this flame.'* What smaller request could he possibly make? He desire not a cup of water, no, nor as much as Lazarus might have held in the palm of his hand, nor yet so much as might have stuck to his whole finger: he only desired a drop from the very tip of it, or not so much only that he would touch his tongue with the tip of his finger a little moistened and cooled with water, and yet this small request would not be granted him. That little, that very little ease, which so small a favour would have given him, was denied him.

This sad story plainly shows us that the torments of the wicked have no intermission, nor decrease, and that those who suffer them shall never obtain the least help or ease, though they want it most extremely, and seek for it with the greatest earnestness and importunity. They shall be like a man that is almost drowned in the midst of the sea, who not finding any firm ground whereupon to set his feet, stretches out his hand every way, and grasps at something with all his might, but still in vain, because there is nothing but water round about him. Thus will it be with those wretches in hell. They are drowning in a bottomless gulf of unspeakable miseries, and they look every way for help, and strive for a little ease; but alas to no purpose, for there is nothing but sorrow, and misery and pain, and horror round about them. And thus it shall be with them, not for a little time, for a month or a year, but for ever and ever, which is a third thing I desire you to observe.

4.3 THERE WILL BE NO DECREASE IN TORMENT

Their pains and torments will be endless as well as easeless, and when they have endured them without any intermission, or decrease, as many years, indeed, ages as there are stars in the firmament, or sands upon the seashore, they shall still be to endure them in the very same manner, as many more. As many more did I say? Yes, ten thousand more. They shall endure them as long as there is a just and holy God to punish them, that is, to eternal ages.

This is but what God himself has told us in plain words; for thus shall the sad sentence run at the great day: *'Depart from me you cursed into everlasting fire'*; and the execution will be accordingly, as we are told, Matthew 25, the last verse. The wicked shall go into everlasting punishment; into punishment that shall be as lasting as the rewards of the righteous, which will be as lasting as God himself.

These are dreadful considerations, my dear Christian friend, and he must be a strange kind of person indeed, and have a heart harder than the hardest gem, that is not mightily affected with them. There are but few people so hardy as to think upon the plagues and judgements of almighty God upon the sinful in this world, without some fear, especially when they think of them as hanging over their own heads and apprehend themselves to be in danger of them. How then can they choose but to tremble at those plagues of another world, which are infinitely more dreadful than the worst of this world?

The evils of the world are particular evils. They afflict but one, or some few parts at once; one disease seizes upon one part and another upon another part. In one disease one sense is pained, and in another, another sense, but never are all the parts and all the senses, at one and the same time, under torment and pain. In this world there is no evil so great but it has its

*'. . . as sweet a thing as life is to us, we wish for
death to deliver us from them.'*

decreases and changes, and therefore no man can be so miserable but he will sometimes have some respite and ease. Let the
evil be never so sharp and pressing, yet the comfort of hope will
not be wanting, and the foresight of a certain end will be a great
relief. Yet notwithstanding this, we many times think the evils
of this world to be intolerable; and, as sweet a thing as life is to
us, we wish for death to deliver us from them. How intolerable

then must the torments of the other world be, which spare no part or faculty of body or soul, which give not the least ease, nor admit of the least decrease, no not for one minute. They exclude all hope of an end, and overwhelm the soul to utter despair of the least remedy! Let our charity lead us sometimes to visit a poor, sick creature and let us observe what pains and agonies he endures for one night: mark how often he tosses and tumbles from one side of his bed to the other; hear how he groans, and what bitter complaints he makes; observe how he counts the hours of the clock, and how long he thinks each hour to be; how passionately he wishes for the dawning of the day, and how tedious the night seems to him.

This we look upon as a sad spectacle, and if we have any heart in us it cannot but melt at it. When we consider that it may be shortly our own case, we are very sensibly touched with it. What shall we think then of the condition of the damned? How deplorable and how miserable must we believe that to be? To be tormented in every member of the body, and every faculty of the soul, with the sharpest and most exquisite torments, and without the least ease or respite. And this not for a night of some few hours, but for an everlasting night, a night that has no morning, and knows no hope of any dawning of the day; to lie in such a night not upon a soft bed (as the sick man does) but in a bed of flames or a hot burning furnace, not at liberty to turn to and fro, and to seek ease, but bound hand and foot. Not with the company of compassionate friends assisting and comforting to the best of their power, but with the horrid company of the damned and accursed spirits, that shall add to the damned's sufferings and sorrows, as much as their power and malice can possibly do.

This must be misery in the height, in its full perfection, if I may so speak. Who trembles not to think of it? Who will not do anything to escape it? Do we fear sickness and pain here in this world? And do not we fear the pains of hell much more? Do we dread a prison and fly from fetters and chains and hazard our very lives to preserve our liberty? Are we not as much afraid of that eternal prison, whose gates shall never be opened when once they are shut upon us, and from which there can be no redemption or deliverance? O dear Christian friend, are we in our right senses or not? Do you think, and do we understand what these things mean? Do they belong to us, or are they meant only for others? Do we take them for the never failing truths of God or for the fables and fancies of brain-sick men? If we understand them not, if we believe them not, why do we call ourselves Christians, and make an outward profession of that which in our hearts we do not approve? But if we understand and believe these things, why do we not tremble at the thoughts of them? Why do we not think about how we may escape them? Why do we not abhor that sin and wickedness which will bring us to them? Why do we not apply ourselves with all our might, and all our care, to the practice of that piety and virtue, which alone through God's mercy, can deliver us from them?

It is an amazing thing, my friend, that these things should make so little impression upon most people, as we find they do. But the Scripture tells us of a God of this world that blinds the eyes and hardens the hearts of men and women and makes them inconsiderate as brutes, otherwise we should be at a loss to give any account of it. We see that they are apprehensive enough of evil in this world, and industrious enough to avoid it. If any evil is great, though it is remote, they dread it. And though its coming is uncertain, yet they take care to prevent it. But alas! As to these unspeakable evils and calamities, they are stupid and inconsiderate as blocks. The least fear of them seems foolish, and the least care and pains to avoid them is thought too much. Surely, friend, there was a time when these evils had greater effects upon the world than they have now, when men and women thought they could not be possessed with too great fear of them, nor take too much care and pains to escape them? Let me show you what a devout father has written concerning some penitents he once saw in a monastery, and then judge what influence these things have had previously and what they ought in reason to have now.

St J. Climas. 9.

When first I came into this monastery I beheld certain things which neither the eyes of the sluggard have ever seen, nor the ears of the negligent heard, nor yet may it be conceived in the heart of any careless and unguided Christians. And afterwards he tells us, how he "saw many penitents standing with their eyes fixed toward heaven, continually calling upon almighty God with tears and sighs for pardon and mercy;" others again, he saw, that "professed they were not worthy to lift up their eyes towards heaven, or to speak to almighty God, and these held their faces down towards the ground, offering their souls in silence to the mercy of God, without speaking so much as one word, as men that had been dumb, full of fear and confusion. Others were clothed in sacks, and hair-cloth, and kneeling with their faces bowed down to their knees, and smiting their foreheads often upon the earth, did bathe the very earth with their tears, and those that wanted tears did lament very grievously, because they wanted them." And after this, he tells us, that "they had death continually before their eyes; and speaking one to another they said, How think you friends? What shall become of us at the dreadful hour? Shall the sentence of condemnation be revoked? Or shall our prayers perchance come into our Lord's ears? Or if they do, how shall they be received? And what profit shall we receive by them? For since they proceed out of such unclean lips, it is to be feared, they might find but little favour in his sight. And much more to this purpose. To which others would answer, as the penitent sinners in Nineveh, Who knows whether the Lord will pardon us, whether he will turn himself to us, and not suffer us to perish. Let us now take courage and persevere continually in crying unto him till the end; for the Lord is merciful, and will be pacified with perseverance. Let us run, my brethren, let us run with all speed, and return to the place from where we are fallen, and let us in no wise pardon this filthy flesh which has undone us; but since it has crucified us, let us crucify it." And then, he proceeds to tell us how hardly they treated their bodies, how they watched and fasted, and punished themselves for their offences against God, insomuch as that "their faces were like the faces of dead men, and their very eyes were sunk into their heads through over-much weakness."

And after all this he tells us how they behaved themselves when any of their brethren lay a dying. They compassed the bed of the dying man, and with earnest and vehement requests, with moving countenances and pitiful words they demanded of him. "How are you brother? How do you feel? What hope do you have? What shall become of you? Have you obtained your long suit? Have you arrived at the haven of your salvation? Have you received any earnest penny of your security? Have you heard any voice within you, which said your sins are forgiven you, your faith has made you whole? Or have you peradventure heard any other voice which said unto you, the wicked shall be turned into hell, and all the nations that forget God, or bind him hand and foot and cast him into utter darkness? What answer do you make, good friend, unto us? Tell us something, we beseech you, that we may understand by you, what is reserved for us; for your suit is now come to an end, and what sentence you shall now receive shall never more be reserved: but our case as yet still depends and looks for sentence."

To which demands some answered. "Blessed be the Lord that has not suffered us to be cast into the teeth of our enemies;" but others after a more doleful manner said, "miserable is that soul that has not fully observed his profession, for now shall he well understand what is prepared for him."

These, my dear friend, were men that did in good earnest

believe the truths of the gospel concerning another world, and being fully persuaded that the punishments appointed for wicked men are most intolerable, were as fully resolved to deliver themselves from them, though by the greatest pains and the severest mortifications. These were men that made use of that faith, and of that reason and understanding which God has given them. Since they thought it prudence to be apprehensive of lesser dangers, they prepared against more considerable evils. They would not, like the unruly horse that starts at a bird and runs himself into a precipice, be fearless of the greatest dangers and suffer themselves to fall into the most insufferable calamities. Are we not concerned, my friend, to do the like, and to make the like use of that faith and reason which God has given us? Does not the fire of hell burn furiously now as ever it did? Have those everlasting torments had any reduced time or period prescribed them? Or are we more able to wrestle with them, or to endure them, than they were?

Or have we any easier way of escaping them discovered to us than was known to them? What easy ways our lusts may find out, I do not know; but sure I am, that there is but one safe and sure way, but one way of God's appointment, which was made known to them as it is to us. That is the way of serving God sincerely, and with all our might, in a holy and virtuous life. If we fail to do this, we shall, as certainly as God is true, be condemned to these everlasting torments. Judge then, dear friend, whether we have not reason to serve God, and whether it is not madness to live in that careless and ungodly way which we see most people do. But now because these things may seem very severe, and possibly occasion in you some hard thoughts of almighty God, I must desire you to consider the following.

C H A P T E R
5

The Rewards Which Have Been Prepared for Us

5.1 God has great rewards for us

ONTAINING A FIFTH ARGUMENT to a holy life, from the consideration of those great rewards God has prepared for good men and women in the other world, the greatness of which may be in some measure estimated.

1. From God's kindness to good people even in this world.
2. That the reward is not proportioned to our deserts, which are very little, but to the goodness of God, which is infinite. And
3. Is designed as the most glorious manifestation of the divine goodness. And
4. It is the purchase of Christ's blood, and the reward of his obedience and sufferings, which are of infinite merit.

The reward, which almighty God has prepared in another world for those that serve him faithfully in this, according to those obligations that lie upon them, both as human beings and Christians. And this gift, I doubt not, will be as pleasant and delightful as the last was sad and dreadful, and will no less declare God's goodness and mercy than that did his justice and severity. I need not tell you that such is our condition, that no reward of right belongs to any services we do. And therefore, be the reward great or little which God has prepared for us, we must acknowledge ourselves indebted to his infinite goodness for it, and that it is on our part altogether undeserved. How much more, then, must we acknowledge ourselves indebted to his goodness (and what a strong obligation should we reckon it to his service) when the reward he has designed for us it not little, like our services, but great, great as we can imagine it to be, as our hearts can desire it should be? To give you a little sight of the greatness of this reward, for it is not possible for you or me to comprehend it fully, I might lead you through a multitude of considerations. But I shall restrain myself to some few, which I think so deserve your serious regard.

5.1.1 GOD IS KIND TO HIS SERVANTS

We cannot but acknowledge that almighty God is very kind to his servants in this world, and there is not one of them can say that he serves God for nothing in this present life. God has given them many good promises, and gives them many good things daily according to those promises.

They have a competent share in all the good things of the world, and such a blessing together with them, as makes them much more sweet and pleasant to them than all the possessions of the wicked. And though they have their afflictions and their trials, yet they have their pleasures and their comforts. They have a peace within which none can disturb, and such joys as none can take from them. I mean the peace of their consciences, and the joys of the Holy Ghost. They are either free from all calamities, or they have such support under them that they are rather matter of joy than sorrow to them. God is good to them at all times in a great measure, but sometimes more abundantly and in a measure extraordinary.

Witness the great things that he has done in all ages for them: What great deliverances he has often given them. What cunning plots and devices against them he has brought to nothing. What wonders he has wrought in their behalf. And how miraculously, when they have been in their greatest distress, he has made them to triumph over all their enemies.

Those who have beheld it have been constrained to cry out in the words of the Psalmist, *'Verily there is a reward for the righteous, doubtless there is a God that judges the earth'* (Psalm 58:11). Now if God deals thus kindly with his servants here, what kindness do you think he will show them hereafter?

If while they are in doing his work he bestows so many good things upon them, what may they expect from him when his work is done? And if in the time of their trial they receive such great benefits from him, what shall they receive (do you think) when their trial is ended and they are fully approved? If such great things are done for their encouragement in his service, what great things are designed (may we believe) for their reward? Especially considering,

5.1.2 God's infinite generosity

That the reward, which God intends for them, shall not be proportioned to the little merit of their services, but to his own infinite goodness: it shall not be such as the services deserve, but such as becomes him to bestow. It is a *gift*, as the apostle tells us (Romans 6:23). And such a gift as shall show the infinite goodness and beneficence of the donor.

5.1.3 God gives on a grand scale

God intends the fullest manifestation of his goodness by his gift, that he may receive everlasting praises, both from people and angels. And how exceedingly great must that gift be? When a prince rewards the services of a poor subject, he considers not so much what his loyal subject deserves as what becomes himself to bestow; and though the service may be but mean, yet he must give as a prince, largely and freely, with respect to his honour. But if a prince design in rewarding a servant to show his magnificence and liberality to the utmost, and to do himself the greatest honour he can, he will give the greatest things his kingdom will afford, and in the noblest and most honourable way.

How great then and how good will that reward be which the king of kings, the supreme ruler and governor of the world, will give to his faithful servants? How little less than infinite must that be, which will become so glorious a majesty to bestow? Especially since he designs to manifest his goodness and bounty in the highest measure? And to let all the world know how much he deserved the love and service of all his creatures. When God, before the foundations of the world, designed to declare his power and wisdom and goodness, what a world did he create! What beautiful heavens! What glittering stars! What elements! And in how marvellous a manner did he unite and compact them together! And yet he intended this vast and beautiful building to last but for a time, and then to be destroyed. And he knew that the noblest of his creatures, which he made to inhabit it, would be rebellious against him, and few of them give him his due honour and obedience.

Imagine, then, what he will do when he designs the utmost manifestation of his almighty goodness in rewarding his faithful servants: what a glorious place will he make for them! What riches and honours will he confer upon them! Will they not be as great as his infinite goodness can bestow? And how incomparably great must we judge this to be! And yet we may consider further,

5.1.4 Christ Purchased Our Reward

This reward designed for God's servants is that which Christ has received from his Father to give them – for all his pains and tears and sweat and blood. That is the purchase of the blood of the Son of God, and the recompense of his obedience to the death. Now how great a reward must so beloved a son deserve by so great and perfect an obedience? Can anything, how ever excellent, be thought too good for him, or too great a recompense for his sufferings? Considering our own poor services, we could not hope for such manifestations of God's goodness as I have spoken of. Yet considering the merits of Christ, we have no reason to doubt them. For if infinite goodness can admit of any motive to show itself to the utmost, this must be the greatest and most prevailing. And yet further, to raise our thoughts one degree higher, we may consider,

5.2 The Reward Will Be Great Because of Christ

Following a prosecution of the same arguments, this reward of good men must be very great because it is not only the reward Christ purchased for his disciples, but that also which he obtained for himself, as the recompense of his obedience and sufferings. And also a more particular explication wherein this happiness consists, a serious expostulation with those who slight it, and the necessity of holiness for the obtaining of it.

5.3 CHRIST ALSO OBTAINED THE REWARD FOR HIMSELF

This reward is not only as the reward which Christ obtained for his servants, but as the reward which he obtained for himself, as the very recompense which his heavenly Father has given him for his obedience. For the Scriptures teach us plainly that it is the very same reward which he has received that his servants shall enjoy. We learn it from his own mouth, in Matthew 25:21, where he bids the faithful servant that had improved his talents to his advantage to enter into the joy of his Lord. And Paul, one of his chosen servants, that knew as much of this matter as any man ever did, has told us the same in Romans 8:17. Here he expressly affirms *'that we are heirs of God, and co-heirs with Christ Jesus.'*

Whatever glory or joy or riches or honours Christ possesses upon the account of his obedience, that shall all his faithful servants enjoy together with him. Has God exalted him for his obedience, and given him a kingdom above all kingdoms? It is as certain that his servants shall be exalted likewise, *'and reign together with him'* (2 Timothy 2:12 and Revelation 22:5).

Is Christ ascended into the highest heavens, and does he dwell in the bosom of his Father? It is as certain that he shall come one day from heaven, and receive all his servants to himself, *'that where he is, they may be also'* (John 14:3). Is that frail and mortal body, which he had while he was upon the earth, and which suffered the pains and torments of the cross, changed into a glorious, immortal, impassible body? It is as certain, *'that the vile bodies of his servants shall be so changed likewise, and fashioned like to his glorious body, according to the working whereby he is able to subdue all things to himself'* (Philippians 3:21).

Is that glory which he is exalted to, that joy and happiness which he is possessed of, never to have an end? It is as certain that the glory and felicity of his servants shall be as lasting; for it is an inheritance incorruptible, undefiled, and that fades not away (1 Peter 1:4). This, dear friend, is the reward of God's faithful servants. And can your heart conceive anything greater, or your soul wish for anything more? Can you conceive what it is to put off this vile mortal body, with all its evil affections, and uneasy attendants – to be freed from all defects and imperfections, from all diseases and distempers, all infirmities and deformities? To be like to the angels in heaven, and having put on incorruption and immortality, to shine like the sun in the firmament in the kingdom of God? Can you conceive what a happiness it will be to be with Christ, to behold the blessed face of that dear person, who does so highly deserve us, both upon the score of his infinite perfections, and likewise upon the account of his inestimable benefits?

Can you conceive what a happiness it will be to *'behold God face to face'*, as St Paul says in 1 Corinthians 13:12? Or to see him as he is, as St John expresses it, in 1 John 3:2? It is to have the most clear and comprehensive knowledge of him that finite creatures can possibly have. To know all his adorable perfections, his almighty power, his incomprehensible wisdom, his eternal justice, his resplendent purity and holiness, his immeasurable goodness and love. And to feel the mighty power of this knowledge upon our souls transforming us into the likeness of God, and uniting our wills most perfectly to him, whereby we shall both possess God, and be possessed by him? Can you conceive what a happiness it will be for millions of millions of such God-like creatures to be inseparably together, and with united hearts and mouths to be continually singing songs of praise to the great God of love, who loved them infinitely and taught them to love him again and one another?

And can you think how much it will add to their happiness

to have a full and perfect assurance, that it shall never have an end, that it shall be as lasting as it is great, and never know the least diminution or decay? I know, friend, that all this is far above the reach of your most raised thoughts. It is too great a happiness to enter into the heart of man, *'as flesh and blood cannot inherit it'* (1 Corinthians 15:50), that is, as man in his present weak and corruptible estate cannot be a partaker of it, so neither can he comprehend it. When we are possessed of it, then and not till then shall we fully understand it.

O blessed God! Why are you thus good to the ungrateful and unworthy? Why have you prepared such a happiness for those who neither consider it, nor seek after it? Why is such a price put into the hands of fools, who have not the hearts to make use of it, who fondly choose to gratify their lusts rather than to save their souls and foolishly prefer the momentary enjoyments of sin and folly before a glorious and happy immortality? Vain and foolish people! How is it that you do not understand your own greatest interest? Why does that reason and judgement, which in other matters constantly attends you, in this – which is of the greatest moment and concernment to you – so strangely fail you? Does not all the world see that you desire and seek after such things as you apprehend to be good, and that you are more or less careful in seeking after such things, according to the value you put upon them, and the esteem you have for them? For a small estate you will take great pains, you will run great hazards, and suffer great hardships. For a great estate you will do and suffer more. For a crown or kingdom yet more. Why then will you not do and suffer as much for this glorious and eternal reward, which far transcends all the riches and the glories of the world?

The author to the Hebrews tells us that Moses despised the riches and honours and pleasures of the court of the Pharaoh for this reward (Hebrews 11:24,25). And that a multitude of wise and holy men have had trial of cruel mockings and scourgings, of bonds and imprisonment, and have suffered patiently, even joyfully, the worst things that wicked men and devils could inflict upon them – because they had their eyes upon it and hoped to obtain it. And St Augustine, I remember, professes that he could be content to do or suffer anything, even to suffer the torments of hell for a time, that he might come to heaven at last. And why is it that we have not as great an esteem for it? Or if we have, why do we not labour, why are we not willing to do and suffer as much for it? Do you think that this care and pains, which I speak of, is needless as to the obtaining of it? Or may we hope for it from God's mercy and goodness without that strict and holy life which I have spoken of? What? Do you believe almighty God is a liar, or that he is not in earnest when he tells you that *without holiness no man shall see Him* (Hebrews 12:14)? Does not a reward necessarily relate to service, and can you expect the reward though you do no service?

Can you imagine that such a reward, a reward so great and glorious, that the very best of us, not withstanding the promises of God, dare hardly presume to hope for, shall be given to those that are slaves to their own lusts, and either serve not God at all, or no farther than their lusts will give them leave? What, is this a reward for apostates from God, for rebels against heaven, for those that desire it not, or value it not, but prefer the pleasures of sin and the profits of the world before it? What? Will it be the same thing as to another world, whether men answer the purpose of their creation or not, whether they dishonour their holy profession by an unholy life or not, whether they love God or not, whether they follow the example of Christ or not, and in one word, whether they are suited for heavenly glory and felicity by pure and God-like dispositions, and the participation of the divine nature – or are ever so unsuited for it, by brutish lusts or devilish qualities and dispositions?

There is a vast difference between heaven and hell no less than there is between light and darkness, between the greatest happiness and the greatest misery. And ought there not to be a vast difference likewise between those that shall enjoy the one, and those that shall fall under the other?

Can a holy and righteous God make so great difference between the eternal estates of men, as to make some eternally happy and others eternally miserable, who differ here one from another in little or nothing, but only in a little outward profession, or the observation of some few rites and ceremonies, or in a formal and civil carriage or demeanour? Surely it is impossible that these things should enter into the head of any sober and thoughtful person, and therefore you must acknowledge the necessity of living a holy life, if you hope for the heavenly glory and felicity. Is not the heavenly glory encouragement enough for you to do so? Will not that make you sufficiently committed to the greatest care and pains you can take, for the worst things you can suffer, or the greatest hazards you can possibly run? Yes, undoubtedly it will. Therefore I leave the exhortation of the apostle with you from 1 Corinthians 15:58, *'Therefore my beloved Brethren, be steadfast, unmoveable, always abounding in the work of the Lord, forasmuch as you know that your labour is not in vain in the Lord.'*

I shall add but one thing more, and I will dispatch it in few words, namely,

REWARDS AND PUNISHMENTS ARE NOT FAR OFF

CONTAINING A SIXTH ARGUMENT TO A HOLY LIFE, FROM
CONSIDERING THAT THESE REWARDS AND PUNISHMENTS ARE
NOT SO FAR OFF AS SOME PERSONS VAINLY IMAGINE.

ONSIDER THESE REWARDS and punishments which I
have spoken of not as things at a great distance from
you, but as they are indeed, and in truth, very near
to you. There is but a little part of a very short life,
of a life which is between you and them.

We have at most but some few breaths to draw before we
must pass into our eternal state, and be either happy or miserable, without any manner of change or alteration for ever.
Death is continually laying his snares for us, and has so many
secret and unknown ways to do his work upon us, that we live
every moment, as it were, by miracle. And it is a much stranger
thing that we have lived till this day, than it would be if we
should die before tomorrow. It is true that we are apt to flatter
ourselves with hopes of long life, but how foolish such hopes
are! The unexpected fall of someone or another every day about
us should convince us.

There are thousands now in their graves that came no
sooner into the world than we, who hoped to live as long as we.
What are we, and what are our hopes, that both may not be cut
off within a few hours? And why may not we make our beds in

the dust as much sooner than we expect as they have done? Now tell me, friend, have you so low an opinion of the heavenly glory and felicity, as that it cannot engage you to serve God so little a time for it? Or have hell's torments so little of terror in them that you cannot resolve to undergo so short a trouble to avoid them? Or is there anything in this world which can make you neglect a matter of so great importance to you, when you think how little a while you can enjoy it? The histories of England tell us of a Saxon queen, that by an innocent and happy piece of policy prevailed with her husband to leave his debaucheries and to live Christianly. She did it like this:

There was a day when the king and his favourites feasted and frolicked in an extraordinary manner. And she, as soon as their mirth was ended, caused the same place to be covered with dung and filthiness and to be made as loathesome as possible. When she had done, she desired the king to go there and to look upon the late scene of their mirth and jollity. When the king was beholding and musing in his mind of the sudden change, she took the opportunity to ask him where all the mirth of the past days was and what footsteps did now remain of it?

She asked him if all such things were not as wind and vanity, which pass away in an instant and are not to be recalled? And with these and the like speeches she taught him to despise the world and to seek after the kingdom of heaven. I shall make no other use of the story than to ask you to reflect upon your life past and to consider what is become of all your former pleasures. I know that they are all past and gone and that the time is coming when as much may be said of all your worldly enjoyments. They will be as far from you and as useless to you as all your past pleasures are now. In the hour of death, and from that hour to all eternity, you may say as was said in the book of Wisdom*, *'What has pride profited us? And what good has riches with all our wanting brought us? All those things are passed away like* *a shadow, or like a rumour that passes by.'*

And therefore be so wise for your own good as to condemn these worthless fugitive things, and for the little remainder of your life to endeavour to make sure of the better and more abiding things which God has prepared for you in heaven.

You have, sometimes perhaps, been visited with sickness and have thought yourself to be upon the borders of the grave. Call to mind, I beseech you, what thoughts then possessed you. Did you not then look upon the world as vanity? And did not all your past follies torment you with a bitter remembrance? Did not the few good things that you had done please you better than all the world? And did you not heartily repent that your whole life was not employed in such good ways? Remember, I beg you, that it will shortly come to that again. The evil day is at hand, and your present delights will be vanished, and your worldly enjoyments will be useless and unprofitable. And if you have not the conscience of a good life to cheer you, you will be miserable without help or remedy. O prepare, prepare, dear friend, for that time, by a holy and Christian life, and let nothing upon earth divert or hinder you. Why should that rob you of your greatest bliss which will not profit you in the least when you have the greatest need of it? Why should that make you miserable for ever, which cannot make you happy for a little time?

---

* The book of Wisdom is from the Apocrypha, a set of intertestimental books (written between the time of the Old and New Testaments) which are considered a part of the canon of Scriptures by Roman Catholics, but not by Protestants. However, up until the time of the puritans in England, most Protestant Bibles, including Luther's, contained the Apocrypha as a separate, non-canonical section. These books were considered wise advice but not the ordained word of God. Bibles in the Church of England, both at the time this book was written, and up to today, continue to contain the Apocrypha as a separate section, but do not include it in the canon of Scripture, nor derive any doctrine from it. Article VI of the Thirty-nine Articles of Religion of the Church of England refers to the Apocrypha thus: 'And the other Books (as Hierome [Jerome] saith) the Church does read for example of life and instruction of manners; but yet doth it not apply them to establish any doctrine.'

Remember your end, said a wise man, and you shall never do amiss. He that knows that he stands upon the brink of eternity is a bold fool if he dares do who so wickedly. He is mad that will commit a crime this day, who knows that before the next he may be bearing the punishments of it in everlasting sorrows.

Thus have I laid before you, dear friend, some arguments and motives to persuade you to a holy life: and so I have brought the first part of my intended work to an end. The things that I have offered to you, I am sure deserve your serious consideration. Let them be considered accordingly, and suffer them to have their due influence upon you, and I shall give you no further trouble in this matter. Weigh them well, and according to the reason you find in them, so do. And I ask no more of you. Live as a man created on purpose by God ought to live – to know and love and serve him here, and to enjoy him for ever hereafter. Live as a man advanced to the knowledge and profession of Christianity is obliged to live. Live as a person is in all reason bound to live that must give an account hereafter of his whole life to a just and impartial judge. Live as one who believes that he shall be unspeakably and eternally miserable if he lives amiss; and that he shall be eternally happy if he lives as he ought.

Live as one that knows that he has but a short life to live, a life that is but a moment in respect to eternity, and that (yet) upon this little moment his eternal state depends. In a word: as a man dying, hastening to the grave, and to the judgement-seat of Christ, and to everlasting bliss or woe, must be concerned to live. Live, thus, dear friend, and I have my desire. Only let me beg your prayers that I may live thus likewise, that both of us may be happy for ever. *Amen, Amen.*

THE END OF THE FIRST PART

PART 2

General Directions on How to Live a Holy and Christian Life

I am now to give you some directions how to live that holy and Christian life, which in the former part of this book, I have endeavoured to persuade you to. It shall be my care not to trouble you with many and less necessary things. And I beg you, that it may be yours to consider what I say impartially and to give it the regard which, upon consideration, you shall find it to deserve. Now, because I suppose you to be convinced that if you would be happy eternally it is necessary that you should live a holy life, the first thing I shall advise you to is

CHAPTER
1
=

TO RESOLVE UPON A HOLY LIFE

CONTAINING THE FIRST ADVICE, SERIOUSLY TO RESOLVE
UPON A HOLY LIFE — AS WELL AS THE NECESSITY OF SUCH A
RESOLUTION, AND THE GREAT VIRTUE AND EFFICACY OF IT.
CONTAINING SOME DIRECTIONS ON HOW TO FORM A
LASTING RESOLUTION.

1.1 *First, to resolve soberly and deliberately, not rashly and in haste, maturely to consider what it is we must resolve, and carefully to examine all the advantages and disadvantages on both sides.*

1.2 *Secondly, to take the matter into consideration several distinct times before we fix our resolution.*

1.3 *Thirdly, to back this resolution with a solemn vow.*

A prosecution of the same argument, containing some further directions in making a lasting resolution.

1.4 *Fourthly, to write down our resolutions in the words wherein we make them, and to engage ourselves to God in a solemn bond and contract.*

1.5 *Fifthly, to make known this resolution to the world, as often as a fit occasion offers, which very much tends to the glory of God, delivers us from many temptations, and makes us more steadfast to what we resolve.*

1.6 *Sixthly, to seek out some good men and women who have taken up the same resolutions, and to contract an intimate friendship and acquaintance with them. Or, if we cannot find any such, to endeavour to persuade our old friends and companions to enter into such a religious friendship.*

1.1 A RESOLUTION WILL STRENGTHEN YOUR CAUSE

Make an absolute and peremptory resolution to live a holy life. 'I see it is necessary that I should do so (may you say). I cannot be happy for ever if I do not live so; and therefore I am resolved I will live so, and nothing shall divert or hinder me.'

Without this peremptory resolution, you will never be able to do what you may desire. You may begin well, but you will fail to persevere to the end. You will be as the double-minded man, which St James speaks of, in chapter 1:8, *'Unstable in your ways.'* You will be of one mind while in the good way, and another while in the bad, according to the circumstances of your life and the sway of your inclinations. But with this resolution begin and prosper. Resolution works wonders every day in other matters, and in this, be confident, it will do much more – because God will bless it. It has a mighty efficacy in itself, and whoever is possessed of it seldom fails to bring his design to pass.

It makes a person intent upon the thing he would do, inquisitive after the best means to effect it, watchful and ready to lay hold upon all fitting opportunities, jealous of the least impediments and hindrances, bold and constant in the midst of difficulties and dangers, and so excludes that forgetfulness and inadvertency, that negligence and sloth, that rashness and levity, that doubtfulness and faintheartedness, which overthrows the good purposes of many, and frustrates their best designs. But how much better will the efficacy of it be, do you think, when it is backed with the almighty grace of God, which in this matter will be ever assisting it? The truth is, your work is half done when you are fully resolved, and if your resolution does not fail, I dare promise you as good success as your heart can wish. But then care must be taken that your resolution continues firm and strong. That it may do so, you must observe the following directions.

1.2 DIRECTIONS ON HOW TO FORM A RESOLUTION

You must make it soberly and deliberately, not rashly and in haste. You must consider what you are about to resolve upon, what difficulties and discouragements you are likely to meet with, and what dangers and inconveniences may attend you in it. And when you have done this, you must consult your own reason and understanding upon these and the like questions:

It is reasonable that I should undertake and resolve upon such a business as this is? Is it possible for me to effect it? Can I march through all the difficulties and overcome all the temptations which may or can befall me in it? Is the design honourable and worthy? And can I hope for a sufficient recompense for all the troubles it will put me to?

For the avoiding of all error and mistake, it will not be amiss for you to put down in writing (if you can) all that you are considering, as also your judgement and determination upon every particular. However, fail not to get as clear and distinct an idea of everything as possibly you can, and let nothing pass you without due consideration. Run through all the parts and duties of a holy life in your thoughts, and tell your heart, 'This I must do; this I must fly from; this I must suffer. Almighty God requires it, and I cannot hope to be excused in anything. Tell me, O my heart (you may say) will you be content if I shall do it or not? Will you not prove false to me if I resolve it?'

These things I must attend to, not for a few days only, or at some certain times and seasons, but constantly and perpetually, throughout the whole course of my life. It must be my business to obey and please God in all my ways, and all my worldly affairs and fleshly pleasures must give place to it. 'Tell me, O my heart, how do you approve of this? Have I your free consent to undertake it? And will you be content that I now begin it?'

Then suppose within yourself the greatest temptations that can befall you, to discourage and draw you aside. Suppose that your mother who bare you in her womb, and nourished you with her breasts, and loves you as her life, should come with weeping eyes to you, and, with the most melting expressions that love and sorrow could put into her mouth, should entreat you to do some wicked act, or to prevent you from doing your duty in any matter. And suppose the wife (or husband) of your bosom, who is as your very soul, should join with her in the same desire, and tell you, as Delilah did Sampson (Judges 16:15), *'How can you say I love you, when your heart is not with me?'* And it may be that your dearest friends and family members will plead with you also for the same thing.

And then you must ask yourself, 'Shall I be able to withstand all these temptations, to resist the pleading of a kind and tender mother, to turn my back upon the wife of my bosom, and to ignore all my friends, rather than sin against God and wound my own conscience?' And further, imagine for yourself the worst things that can befall someone in this world. Suppose you must lose all you have in the world, yes, and your very life, if you will not sin against him. Suppose you must suffer the sharpest reproaches, and the most cruel death that ever was invented, if you will be faithful to him, and do your duty.

And then charge your heart to tell you, whether it will not sink at such a trial, and basely betray you to sin and shame.

These are hard things indeed, and the bare thoughts of them are dreadful. How much more will the things themselves be, when you come to try them? But what good thing was ever obtained without some difficulty? And what wise man was ever discouraged with difficulties, that was sure of a recompense far exceeding the worst troubles he could possibly undergo? Is it not reasonable that I should do and suffer anything that my God shall impose upon me?

Should not that life and being which he has given me be altogether at his service? May not my dear and loving Saviour justly expect as much from me, since he has purchased me with his most precious blood? Did he not undergo much more for my sake than he requires me to do for his? And may not that joy which encouraged him be a just encouragement for me? Will not heaven make amends for all, and justify my choice and resolution to all the world? What if I am weak and frail? What if there are many subtle enemies to my undertaking? Is not he that is with me greater than all that are against me? Cannot the spirit of my God make my weakness strong, and cause me to triumph over all my adversaries? Has he not done as much for millions of such weaklings as I am? Have not many before us taken up the very same resolution, and in spite of all the powers of darkness and their accursed instruments made it good to the last minute of their lives? I know, I know, my God and Saviour will not fail me in so good an undertaking, and he will make my weakness to redound to the glory of his grace. Therefore I may, I must, I will, I *do* resolve upon a holy life.

Thus I do advise you to consider things before you do resolve, that your resolution may be the work of your whole soul, that your understanding may fully approve of it under the most disadvantageous circumstances, and your will entirely embrace it, and that nothing may befall you in your afterlife that may stagger you as not foreseen, or cause you to question the wisdom of your undertaking. And this advice (you must know) is not the mere issue of my own brains, but the counsel of our great and good Master in two plain parables, Luke 14:28-32 – *'Which of you intending to build a tower, does not sit down and count the cost, whether he has sufficient to finish it? Lest happily after he has laid the foundation, and is not able to finish it, all that behold it begin to mock him, saying, this man began to build, and was not able to finish it. Or what king, going to make war against another king, sits not down first and considers whether he is able with ten thousand to meet him that comes against him with twenty thousand, or else while the other is yet a great way off, he sends an ambassador and desires conditions of peace.'*

Parables plainly tell us that no wise man will begin to build but who sees that he shall be able to finish. And no wise king will begin a war without first considering his ability to go through with it. Nor can anyone be thought wise that will take upon himself to be a disciple of Christ, and to follow him in a holy life, before he has well considered what he undertakes, and what trouble and danger it may cost him. The fruits of such rash and unadvised undertakings can ordinarily be no other than shame and sorrow. If religion is once thoroughly wrought into the heart (which will not be done in an hour or two, and can be done by no better way than by frequent meditations), it will in all probability keep possession of it for ever. And if a man is once resolved upon the practice of piety and virtue from a full conviction of the goodness and reasonableness of it, he will hardly be turned aside from it by any temptation. However, if it is admitted into the borders or the skirts of the soul only, to possess only the fancy or imagination, and by the help of these alone does warn the affections, it will in a little time be cast off and all the good purposes which it may for the present produce, will, upon the least alteration of circumstances, be forgotten or laid aside.

Therefore in the second place, I shall commend to you that you do not fully determine, and fix your resolution upon just one consideration or deliberation (however seriously you have done it) but that you take the matter twice or thrice into consideration, after some intermissions – for you will thereby discern whether your resolution is the effect of your judgement, and your entire choice, or whether it is merely of a good temper of body apt to receive religious impressions and a kindly heat, kindled by the working of your imagination.

If it is the good temper and warm imagination that dispossess you to it, you will be of another mind after you have slept or been dealing in other matters. But if it proceeds from the better principle but now mentioned, then what you approve of this day, you will approve of tomorrow and for ever. The more you consider things, the better you will like your intended resolution, and the more ready you will be fully and finally to fix it. What you have considered one day, my counsel is that you take a review of it the next day. Consider afresh what you are to do, consider the pleasures which you must forsake and the difficulties you must undergo. And if, after all, you find yourself sincerely bent to serve the Lord in a holy and Christian life, and no objection offers itself which you perceive your heart to stumble at, then fix your resolution, resolve fully, peremptorily and irrevocably.

And that it may have all the strength which we can possibly add to it, let me advise you further.

1.3 TAKE A SOLEMN VOW

Back it with a vow, with a solemn protestation to almighty God, to keep it firm and steadfast to the end of your life, for as long as any sense of God remains upon your soul. You will thus dread the not-doing of that which by a solemn promise to God you have bound yourself to do – it being in the opinion of all mankind a most abominable thing to falsify our vows and oaths to God, and deserving the severest vengeance that can fall upon the heads of wicked men.

1.4 WRITE DOWN THE RESOLUTION

And further, when you have done this, it will not be amiss to write down your resolution in the very words you have made it, adding likewise the year, and month, and day, wherein you thus engaged yourself; and to keep it by you, as a thing of great concern to you, and once a month at least to look seriously upon it, saying to your heart, 'See, O my heart, what you have done, observe the bond which you have laid upon yourself: it is your own act and deed. There is no disowning it or excepting against it. As sure as I now see it with my eyes, it is recorded before God in heaven, and it shall one day be brought forth against me to my everlasting condemnation if I do not discharge and satisfy it. Go on, O my heart, go on, as you have begun, to keep your resolution firm and to pay your vows unto the most high. And be confident that the Lord will prosper your good desires and endeavours, and reward you according to his gracious covenant and promise, with everlasting glory and felicity.'

1.5 ANNOUNCE YOUR RESOLUTION TO THE WORLD

All this being done, I think you may do well to make known your resolution to the world, as often as fitting occasions may be offered you, that is, as often as God may receive honour by it, or yourself be secured from temptation or sin. Such occa-

Nor can anyone be thought wise that will take upon himself
to be a disciple of Christ, and to follow him in a holy life,
before he has well considered what he undertakes,
and what trouble and danger it may cost him.

sions, in this age, you will frequently meet with. Sometimes you will fall into the company of evil people who dishonour the holy religion which they profess by their wicked and ungodly lives, and they will not spare to reproach you for not running with them into the same excesses and debaucheries. Then you may do well to tell them that you are fully resolved against such practices, and that you did long since take upon you a vow which allows them not, as they have also done; a profession of obedience to the doctrine, and of conformity to the example of the pure and holy Jesus; and that you cannot without gross hypocrisy and inexcusable folly act so contrary to it as they do.

Such a declaration will honour your Lord and Master and shame evildoers, if they are not past all shame and all hope of amendment. Sometimes again, you will meet with men and women that will play the devil's part, and use all their cunning to persuade you to some sinful act. Such people you must let know without delay that you are in the full purpose of your heart as well as in outward profession a Christian, and that you are resolved to serve your Lord and Master to your death, and never do anything which you shall know will in the least displease him. That however light a matter others may make it to disown him by their works, whom with their mouths they own and flatter, yet you esteem it so base and shameful a thing that by the help of God's grace, you have determined never to be guilty of it. And that you cannot but believe it to be as bad, no, much worse, to be false to God than to be false to men. They who do not think so, do most unworthily prefer vile dust and ashes before the high and holy God of heaven and earth.

This must needs stop the mouths of the most impudent tempters, and when you are known to the world to be thus well resolved, you will find a happy freedom from temptations by it. Your old companions in sin (if you have had any) will cease to importune you, and the devil, in despair of success, will seldom trouble you. You will also disarm him of one of the most dangerous weapons by which he destroys the soul of men. You will turn it against himself and make that to be the instrument of your safety, which might have been the instrument of your ruin. By this I mean the fear of reproach from wicked men. (This fear keeps thousands in bondage to sin all their days, going on in their wonted courses, not because they approve, or are truly pleased with them, but because they are ashamed to amend them.)

This reproach, which you have courageously condemned by publicly owning your resolution, will be of little account to you afterwards. For as a resolute soldier – that has passed through the hardest service against the enemy without wound or scar – feels no fear within himself of that which remains, so it will be with you. Having borne the first reproaches of an ungodly world, which are ever the most bitter, you will readily condemn and set at nothing the rest. The only fear of reproach which will then remain in you will be only that which is just and good, namely the fear of deserved reproach for not making good that resolution which you have declared to the world. The greater your fear of this is, the safer and the happier you will be.

Objection. Against this part of my advice I know but one thing that can be objected, namely, that in case you should fail to make good your resolution after this, returning to your former wickedness or carelessness as many, perhaps, have done after they have intended to do well, you will bring shame upon yourself and dishonour to your holy religion.

Answer. And true it is, my friend, that these will be the effects of your failing, and it is as true that great care ought to be taken that nothing be done which will produce so great an evil as either of those. But it is not necessary that you should fail this. It is not probable, if you use that sincerity, consideration, caution and circumspection which I have commended to you –

because of the sufficient grace of God, which will never fail you. Thus the force of the objection lies not against all resolving or owning your resolution, but against doing it rashly and unadvisedly, proudly and vaingloriously. It only admonishes us to proceed with great deliberation and prudence, and to forbear the public owning of it, till we have had some proof of our sincerity towards God, by the discharge of our several duties, and the resistance of some of the more dangerous temptations – especially if we know ourselves to be of a hasty temper and not very constant in other things.

But this being secured, I doubt not but you will find my advice good, and I proposed it to you because of the abounding wickedness of the age. For, though many people call themselves Christian, and think themselves affronted if they are not so esteemed, yet true Christian piety is owned by very few. It is become as disgraceful truly to practise it or to plead for it (more is our misery) as it is to disown it. And therefore we take it to be as much our duty now thus to claim the cause of it against the vile practices of those who foolishly reproach and persecute it – even while they call themselves Christians – as it was of old the duty of Christians to own the name and profession against the persecutions of the heathen and unbelieving world.

Certain it is that Christ is as well confessed by maintaining and defending that real holiness which he came to implant in the hearts and lives of men, as he is by the belief and acknowledgement of those things which he was pleased to do and suffer for our sake.

Therefore, the denying of our obligation to his holiness, or of our resolution to embrace and live in it, whenever we have a just cause to own it, is as truly a denying of Christ as is our protesting, when in danger, that we know him not. Be not afraid nor ashamed then to make yourself known to the world to be in the resolution of your heart a true Christian, that Christ may not be ashamed of you before the angels of God, in that day when all the secrets of our hearts shall be made manifest.

Those vile wretches that live to the dishonour of him whose name they are called by, and to the reproach of human nature, do not blush (as you may observe) to make known the baseness of their designs and the lewdness of their actions. They commit their wickedness in the sight of the sun, and are not ashamed to boast of it.

Should you be ashamed to live worthy of Christ, to be truly a son of God, and to have a design upon glory and immortality? No, let them be ashamed that do shameful things. But for you, your design is honourable and worthy of a man, and your resolution is becoming a Christian, and it is necessary to you, being one. There is a shame, we are told, that ends in death. Surely this is that: when men and women are ashamed of that which is truly their glory – and they dare not be what they know they ought to be – because they may be reproached by evil people when they are known to be so.

1.6 SEEK OUT LIKE-MINDED PEOPLE

There is but one thing more to be added in this matter, namely, that you will do well to seek out some good people that have taken up the same resolution, and to acquaint yourself with them, and if possible to make them familiar and bosom friends. Let them know your design and purpose of living a holy and Christian life. Tell them what esteem you have for them, because you perceive that they intend to do no less. Beg their good opinion, and their love according as they shall behold the sincerity and reality in the vows you make. Desire their prayers, their instruction, their reproofs, their encouragements, according as they shall see you stand in need of them. And ask that they will look upon you as a poor and unworthy member of that holy body to which they belong and of which Christ is the head – that holy body that hopes by the mercy of God to be glorified with Christ one day. They will therefore have that regard and tenderness for you which the members of the same body have for one another. Desire them to accept the like regard and love from you, and of all the good offices that true Christian charity can enable you to do for them.

I confess it will be no easy matter for you to find such persons. The number of them is but small, and they are generally no great pretenders, but modest and reserved, and perhaps more reserved, all things considered, than they ought to be. The vile hypocrisy of pretenders to holiness in this last age, and the daily abuse of its good name by men and women that seek themselves in the ruin of the Church, may seem to encourage their closeness, and desire of being unknown. But the growth of atheism and profaneness which those false pretences have occasioned, and the danger we have fallen into – of losing those great advantages of the practice of piety which our Church affords us does more strongly require the sincere to lay open that piety which they practise in secret, and to let the world know by their actions that there are some that own the cause of real holiness without hypocrisy and guile.

And let me tell you that if good men of this Church will thus show themselves, and unite together in the several parts of the country, disposing themselves into fraternities, or friendly societies, and engaging each other in their several and respective combinations, it will be helpful to one another in all good Christians ways. It would also be the most effectual means for restoring our decaying Christianity to its primitive life and vigour, and the supporting of our tottering and sinking Church.

But, not to lead you too far from the matter I was about, if you can find any of these good people I have spoken of, I charge you to let your heart cleave unto them, and let there not be the least strangeness between you.

Be all as one person (thus it was with the primitive Christians, see Acts 2) and so march forward in the good ways of God against all opposition, observing and *'considering one another, to provoke unto love and to good works'* as the apostle's expressions are (Hebrews 10:23-24), having an eye continually to the captain of our salvation, who has entered into heaven — despite all the powers of darkness — and is there preparing a place for us. You will be no sooner engaged with these good people in love and friendship but you will begin to feel the advantages of it. You will be afraid of no discouragements when you have got the assistance of so many true friends, and you will never fall back from that resolution which has been the occasion of engaging you in such good company. If you forget yourself at any time, you will not be without a reminder, and whenever you fail you will find a restorer. When you are seized with any coldness or dullness, they will be ready to warm and quicken you.

These are advantages so considerable that you cannot prudently care about any pains it may cost you to procure them. And if you cannot be so happy as to be acquainted with any of these good people, you must do as much as lies in you to make some of your old acquaintances good by engaging them in the same resolution which you have taken up yourself.

To this purpose you must make use of all the knowledge you have of them, and the interest you have in them. Tell them what you are resolved upon, with the grounds and reasons of your resolution, and urge them to consider them seriously and impartially. If they approve of what you have done, press them to do the same. If they have aught to object against it, answer their objections and remove their prejudices. If you cannot work upon them at one time, try what you can do at another, and watch for the fittest seasons for your purpose. If one way of discoursing will not take effect, try what another way will do, and remember to fit yourself to their tempers and dispositions so far as innocently you may. If reason will not prevail, try pleading – but to all endeavours with them fail not to add prayers to God for them. In a word, press them with arguments and love and press almighty God with prayers in their behalf, and be confident that sooner or later you shall move according to your heart's desire.

One person thus gained will make you amends for all your pains, for besides the fact that he may prove to be a friend to you, as would those that entered upon a holy life before you, yet he will be a far greater comfort to you than any of them – because in all the good he does, you will have some kind of share. Every step he takes in those good ways you have brought him to will be as a new pledge to assure you of your future glory. There being no greater promises made to any than to those 'who turn to righteousness from the error of their ways' (Daniel 12:3). But enough has been said of framing and fixing your resolution, and the things which I can conceive to be requisite for making it firm and effectual. It is now time that I direct you how to put it in practice, and therefore,

CHAPTER
2
##

SELF-DENIAL

2.1 *Containing the second advice, To take up our cross and forsake all to follow Christ, wherein is explained the nature of this duty, and the necessity of it.*

2.2 *Containing several arguments to reconcile us to this duty of self-denial for our spiritual life and health, from the example of our Saviour, who was a great pattern of self-denial. And from the reasonableness of this duty considered in itself, and the great advantages of it.*

2.3 *Containing some directions how to put this duty of self-denial in practice.*

2.1 TAKE UP YOUR CROSS AND FORSAKE ALL

OU MUST DENY YOURSELF, take up your cross, and forsake all. This is the first thing that is to be done by those that are resolved upon a holy and Christian life, and it is so necessary to be done in the first place, that if you fail in it, will be a vain thing for me to offer you any further direction. Now it is so important that you be persuaded of this truth, that you must allow me leave to show you that I tell you no more in this case than what our blessed Lord and Master has done, in Luke 9:23-24 — *'He said to them all, if any man will come after me, let him deny himself, take up his cross daily, and follow me; for whoever will save his life shall lose it, but whosoever will lose it for my sake, the same shall save it.'* The meaning of which words is plainly this: all those that would be Christians indeed must deny themselves, take up their cross and follow Christ, and not reserve so much as their very lives, but be willing and ready to resign up all for him.

But lest we should imagine this to concern some choice persons only, whom he designed to bring to greater perfection such as his apostles may be thought to be – he was pleased to speak as much, at another time, to the multitudes that followed him, in Luke 14:25,26,27 – *'There were great multitudes with him, and he turned and said unto them, if any man come to me, and hate not his father and mother, and wife and children, and brothers and sisters, yes and his own life also, he cannot be my disciple; and whosoever does not bear his cross and come after me, cannot be my disciple.'* That is, he that will not deny and forsake (as we are wont to do things we hate) whatsoever is *dear* to him in the world, be it father and mother, or wife and children, brothers and sisters, preferring Christ before them all, and is not fully resolved and prepared to suffer anything, however hard, for Christ's sake, cannot be a disciple of Christ, or a true Christian.

The word *'cannot'* signifies such an impossibility as implies a contradiction. To deny ourselves, and all our dearest interests in this world, is essential to the sincere profession of Christianity, and therefore anyone who will not do this cannot be a Christian. Those dear things which he cannot renounce will not allow him to take this profession upon him. Or if he does take it upon him, they will in time cause him to repent his undertaking and to fall away with shame from it.

And then in the words following, he advises them to consider seriously what they are about to do before they took upon themselves to be his disciples. And that his advice might sink more deeply into their minds, he expresses himself in two parables (which I have before mentioned) namely (Luke 14:28-31) of a man intending to build a tower, and sitting down first to consider the cost, and of a king going to make war against another king, and considering first his abilities to go through with it. And then he concludes Luke 14:33, *'So likewise, whosoever he be of you, that forsakes not all that he has, he cannot be my disciple.'*

This conclusion makes it plain: we cannot wisely nor safely engage ourselves to Christ, or enlist ourselves as soldiers under his banner, till we have denied, renounced, given up all interest in ourselves, and whatsoever is dear unto us. Not thus prepared, we do but exasperate and provoke an enemy, our old enemy the devil, whose forces we shall not be able to withstand – and so we lay a foundation for our future shame and ruin. At first reading we may think those comparisons from Luke but ill applied – for what agreement is there between riches and armies, and forsaking all that we have?

Yet upon second thought, we may perceive a very wise design in it. For Christianity is a spiritual warfare, and some of the most powerful enemies we are to encounter are the riches and pleasures and honours of this world, and therefore the strength and courage of a Christian soldier, whereby he will obtain a glorious victory, consist in self-denial and a contempt of this world. And a Christian is God's building, or spiritual house, the temple of God. The very foundation of this building is laid in humility and self-denial, from where proceed all those divine graces and virtues which both complete and adorn the building. These make humility and poverty of spirit, renouncing the love of this world and the very possession of it too in some cases, as necessary to our becoming Christians as a great deal of money is necessary to erect and finish a stately and magnificent building. This appears to be a great truth, and no groundless fancy, as proven by the parable of the wedding supper in the former part of the chapter, which you may do well to reflect upon:

The master sent his servants to call them that were bidden,

when his supper was ready, but they all refused, and desired to be excused. One had bought a piece of ground, and he must go and see it. Another had bought five yoke of oxen, and he must go and prove them. Another had married a wife and he could not come. But when he sent his servants to call the poor, the blind and the lame, they came in immediately so that the poor and miserable people of the world, that have no worldly thing to trust to, or those who have these things but have conquered the love of them, are better disposed to receive the gospel and to become Christians than the rich and the great. The rich and the great have the world at will, as we say, and wallow in the pleasures thereof.

We have a very remarkable instance of the mischief that worldly riches do to those that both have and love them, in the tenth chapter of St Mark's Gospel, and the 17 and 18 verses and following. There are several things in the chapter, relating to it, that deserve our regard. In the verses before we find our blessed Saviour displeased with his disciples for forbidding little children to be brought unto him, and saying to them, *'Suffer little children to come unto me, and forbid them not, for of such is the kingdom of God.'* That is, their innocency and simplicity, their willingness to be guided and sustained by others, makes them the fittest emblems of those that do truly belong to his Church and kingdom. And then he adds, *'Verily I say unto you, whosoever shall not receive the kingdom of God as a little child, he shall not enter therein.'* That is, he that will not take the Christian profession upon him as a little child – that is, with that very humility, disinterestedness, self-denial and resignation as is remarkable in little children – will never submit to those laws which he gives to the world, and shall never be received by him as a Christian.

Now immediately upon this, as if divine providence had designed it for a confirmation of this truth, there came a young man to Christ, upon a very weighty and important business.

This young man's heart was in a good measure set upon eternal life, and he had entertained a great opinion of Christ, as appeared by the haste he made, by the humility of his carriage, and the words he used to him (Mark 10:17): *'He came running, and kneeled to him, and asked him saying, Good Master, what shall I do to inherit eternal life?'* He had done much in order to gain it before. *'He had kept the Commandments from his youth up,'* so he professed, and there is no doubt but he spoke what he thought, and what he had done in a good measure, for it is said verse 21 that *'Jesus loved him'*, that is, he approved of his good beginnings, and desired that they might be perfected. But when he told him that there was one thing still wanting, namely, that he *'must go and sell all, and give to the poor, and take up his cross and follow me'*, the forward young man disliked his counsel, became sad and went away grieved. And why? *'Because he had great possessions.'* He had them and he loved them likewise; and who can blame him for being sad when he was told that to have eternal life he must part with them?

He had not got his riches by fraud and deceit, by violence and oppression, as many among us have done and resolve to keep them (for if so, he had not kept the commandments, which Christ spoke to him of). His love of the world had not prevailed so far upon him as to draw him to such wickedness, but his fault was that he had so great a love of his riches that he could not find it in his heart to part with them, even for the obtaining of everlasting life.

Had he been as a little child, and had valued them no more than a child would have done, he would have obtained his desire and have entered into the kingdom of God. But because it was not thus with him, his good meanings miscarried and he fell short of that happiness which he sought after.

Thus was this unhappy man a sad instance of the truth of our blessed Saviour's words. And so the disciples looked upon him, being astonished at the bewitching power of worldly possessions, but they were astonished to see a man that meant so well, and was come so near to the kingdom of God, overthrown by his great possessions. And since riches had so great a power over him and could turn him back from the kingdom of God, they believed they would turn all the rich men in the world from it. For he, after having kept the commandments from his youth up, trusted in his riches. Thus no rich man could be found, they thought, that they did not trust in them, and therefore said among themselves, in Mark 10:26, *'Who then can be saved?'*

And though Peter immediately expressed some hope of his salvation, and the salvation of his fellow disciples, because they had left all and followed him, yet it appears from what follows in the chapter from verse 35 that he was deceived in his opinion of what they had done. For though they had left their possessions to follow him, yet there was something of selfishness still remaining in them and to be renounced by them. They had too great an opinion of the world's grandeur and they aimed at it more than they should. And this their Master was very well aware of, and therefore he tells them in another place, Matthew 18:3 (when they had proposed a question to him which showed the inclinations of their hearts, asking him, *'Who is the greatest in the kingdom of heaven?'*). *'That except they were converted and became as little children'*, that is, as unconcerned for that greatness which they thought of as little children are, *'They should not enter into the kingdom of heaven.'*

They were converted in a good measure then, and had given a good evidence of it by quitting their possessions for their master's sake. But it seems there was still something to be done. They were not so estranged from the world, nor so resigned as to all fleshly interest, but they needed to be put in mind that they must deny themselves more entirely, *'and become as little children'*. Then would they be fit for that service he designed to put them upon, and not till then. And thus, indeed, it was with them. For while their heads were possessed with fancy that their master was to be a mighty temporal prince, and their souls were hankering after the glories which they imagined they should partake of with him, they were often offended with his discourse. And when they saw him in the hands of his enemies and began to suspect the ruin of their hopes and expectations, they shamefully deserted him.

Thus in St Mark's Gospel, when he began to tell them that *'he must suffer many things and be rejected of the chief priests and elders and scribes, and be put to death'*, Peter *'took him and rebuked him'* (Mark 8:32). And when those things were coming upon him which he spoke of, *'They all forsook him and fled'* (Mark 15:40). Afterwards, when their mistakes were rectified and they were more perfectly purged from the love of earthly things – by the descent of the Holy Spirit upon them – every word that their Master had spoken to them and which the Spirit brought to their remembrance was dear to them, and they were not afraid nor ashamed to confess him before their greatest enemies.

Then the cross of Christ was their greatest glory, and the great desire and joy of their hearts was to be made like to him in suffering and patience and resignation to God. Then they could call upon men to deny themselves and forsake all as earnestly as their Master had done before them. For what else do those repeated exhortations signify, of not living to ourselves, of dying to our sins, of being crucified to the world, of being crucified, dead and buried with Christ, of offering ourselves sacrifices to God, and many more the like, which we read in their epistles? And, indeed, they did it very effectually while their doctrine and practice went hand in hand together. For, in spite of the wickedness of the world and the subtle malice of the devil, they prevailed in all places and filled every corner of the world with the wonders of self-denial, and patience, and contempt of the world; with men that could take joyfully the spoiling of their goods, as we read Hebrews 10:34.

They counted not their lives dear for Christ's sake and the gospel. And such self-denying men were Christians generally in the first ages of Christianity. Witness Athenagoras, who speaking of those of his time, tells us:

> We are not moved with the loss of our estates which our enemies wrest from us, nor with the violence that is offered to our credit and reputation, or if there be anything of greater concernment than these. For although these things are mightily prized and valued among men, yet can we but despise and slight them? No, we can only when beaten refrain from striking again, and make no resistance against those that invade and spoil us, but to those that smite one cheek we can turn the other, and to them that take away the coat we can let go the cloak also.

Thus did the apostles and first Christians deny themselves and forsake all. And are not we bound to do so likewise, do you think? May we be his disciples upon easier terms than they were? Has he made the way to heaven broader than it was, and given us allowances which he did not give them of former ages? Certainly not.

It is true that we are not altogether in the same circumstances as they were in, for the Christian profession (though now honourable among us) was then so vile a thing in the eyes of the world, and so extremely hated, that none could take it up and own it publicly without hazarding the loss of all they had. Therefore, if any were so rash as to take it up before they had denied themselves, they quickly discovered their rashness and want of self-denial by falling away from it. It must be granted that self-denial is not now so necessary to the taking up and retaining of the mere profession of Christianity as it was of old. But then as to the *practice* of it, it is certainly as necessary as ever it was – and though the profession be honoured at present, yet the practice is as much despised, and doing what we profess, in a pure and holy life, will as certainly expose us to as many evils (God be thanked that I cannot say 'to death') as the profession of old was used to do. Therefore, he that will satisfy that Name which he has taken upon him, and observe the profession which he has made in baptism, must be brought to that frame and temper of mind which those good men and women in the beginning of Christianity were brought to. That is, they must take off from themselves all self-interests and self-satisfactions. They must renounce all propriety in themselves and everything else, be dead to the world, and have no more affection to the worldly things than the dead have. All that so nothing may hinder them from living unto God.

There are but few indeed that seriously consider this, and therefore we see that people generally account themselves Christians from their baptism. And as long as they do not renounce their baptism, they are confident that they are so. But he has told us that many are called (that is, to be Christians), but few are chosen. Those who only profess themselves to be so, he makes another judgement of them. And they will know it one day to their shame and sorrow. They have fallen by God's good providence upon that which is in fashion among us, and they see at present no reason why they should call it off – I mean the outward profession of Christianity. But as for that which is not fashionable and in credit, that is the denying of ourselves and dying to the world – they never understood it. And because they do not deny themselves and die to the world, they cannot live to God.

This might suffice, my friend, to convince you that you must deny yourself and forsake all if you desire to live a holy and Christian life. Because I know of our unwillingness to entertain this hard saying (as they are apt to term it), and because I know that it is so absolutely necessary that those who will live a Christian life do both believe and practise it, I shall show you yet further that not considering or not practising this self-denial has been the main cause why so many have rejected the gospel in all ages. And it is why so many of these that have seemed to receive it have yielded so lame and so imperfect an obedience to it. Did you never read in your Bible how few of those that heard Christ preach while he was upon the earth, and saw the miracles that he wrought, especially of the greater sort, did truly believe in him? Have any of the rulers or of the Pharisees believed on him? This was a choking question to any that would dare to speak for him (John 7:48). Those few disciples that he had were of the poorer sort of people that had not much to trust to, or much to lose for his sake. If any of the richer or greater sort were convinced that he was the Christ, then they did not dare to own it. They would go by night and in secret to tell him of their faith, but publicly and openly they professed it not. And what might be the reason for this, do you think?

Had not these great men those natural powers of judging, of assenting and consenting to the truth, which the others had? Was not their natural courage as great, and would they not have showed it as much in other cases, as these poor people could have done? Yes, undoubtedly. In all other matters they were the wise, and the others the ignorant; they the bold and the hardy, the others the poor spirited and cowardly. But in this case the wise were fools, and the courageous mere cowards. And how was this? Those great rich and proud men could not – or would not – learn this one lesson. It would have opened their blind eyes, and have raised their poor spirits, to that degree of boldness, which they beheld in the disciples of Christ, and wondered at. *'How can you believe* (said Christ himself to them) *as long as you receive honour from one another, and see not the honour that comes from God only?'* (John 5:44). They loved themselves, and the praise of men too well, to approve of anything that would lessen their reputation in the least, or bring them one step lower in the esteem of the world. And they were too covetous, as appears from other places of Scripture, to leave all to follow one that had not a house to put his head in. Did you never observe the monstrous unbelief of many among us and the gross hypocrisy of others? Did you never observe what great opposition is made by some people against some of the clearest truths of Christianity, who yet seem very fond of other truths that are not so clear and are not so open to human understanding?

And did you never take notice how strict some people are in some things who yet allow themselves to violate very plain and very weighty precepts? As for instance the doctrine of the Trinity we see unanimously acknowledged by many thousands among us, when the divine authority of Christ's ministers, and the right of their wages meets with many opposers in all places. And some people can preach and pray from morning till night, and talk Scripture to each other with much seeming seriousness, when like the Pharisees of old they will embrace any fair chance to devour the house of a poor widow or orphan or to exalt themselves somewhat higher in the world. And what do you think is the reason of these things? The same, without doubt, that hindered the Jews of old from receiving Christ. And if these truths which they profess to believe, and these Christian duties which they follow, did as much to oppose their worldly interests and fleshly lusts as the acknowledging of Jesus to be the Christ opposed the interests and lusts of the unbelieving Jews, then they would quickly fall away from those truths and those duties, if not also from the whole religion.

Not that I believe that they have merely pretended when they first professed Christ, or that they are and have been so zealous in some things merely for worldly ends. I doubt not but many of them have meant well from the very beginning. But those naughty and corrupt affections, which being renounced by Christ, did so fatally prejudice the Jews against him, do as strongly prejudice these professed Christians against the great part of his doctrine. Those corrupt affections, which they should have renounced at their first setting out, are like a thick cloud upon the eyes of their minds, not allowing them to discern those truths which to genuine Christians are as manifest as the sun at noonday. These corrupt affections are a strong bias upon their wills, drawing them aside from those good paths which they have a desire to walk in. These people intend well in the general, like the rich man when he came to Christ, and they do well in those things that do not oppose their inordinate affections. But when they are to learn those duties to which their lusts will not be reconciled, either they are not able to understand them or have not the power to practise them. They are like the wolf in the fable, that was sent to school to read, could make no word of all the letters, but could only see in them lamb – because of his appetite for the flesh of that harmless creature. They also can see nothing but what they lust after.

I will conclude therefore (and I think I have good reason for it) that if we desire and are resolved to be Christians, we must in the first place renounce ourselves, and entirely put off our carnal lusts and worldly affections. Our desires and resolutions will be vain and come to nought if we fail to do it. We may intend well and perhaps do many good things. And we may make a fair show for a while, and mount up to heaven in our own thoughts and in the opinion of the world. But like as an unwise builder that raises a very fair structure upwards, not having laid a good and firm foundation, and who will in a little time be convinced of this error by its ruin, so when a time of trial and temptation comes to us, our own fall will show us our error. When the winds blow and rains fall, and the floods come, our pretty frame of religion will come to ruin, and our high hopes will perish together with it.

Now after this, I suppose, I need to tell you that I have insisted so much upon this particular with great reason.

2.2 CHRIST IS NOT A HARD MASTER

It remains that I endeavour briefly to create in you a good opinion of the duty I have been speaking of, and to show you that it is not such an unreasonable thing as some people imagine it, to be obliged to it, and that Christ cannot reasonably be thought a hard master for laying it upon us. For surely,

2.2.1 HE REQUIRES NOTHING FROM US BUT WHAT IS NECESSARY

He that has laid nothing upon us, but what our state and condition, and his own design of love and mercy towards us, did make necessary, cannot be judged hard or cruel to us. And has Christ required anything more in this matter? No, undoubtedly he could not give us health and life (however much he desires it) without removing our desires. He could not be the author of salvation to us without taking away that which was our ruin and destruction. And what was our disease and ruin but an inordinate and immoderate love of ourselves and our fellow creatures – whereby we fell away from God, to be as gods ourselves, to please ourselves, to provide for ourselves to do our own wills, and to satisfy our own desires without restraint or control?

Now, what is it that we would have, when we quarrel with Christ, and call this commandment grievous? Would we have our health and our diseases too? Would we live and die also? Would we serve God a little and ourselves much more? Or would we serve him so far only as we shall please ourselves, and have that be taken for all the service that we owe him? If you think this to be unreasonable, as you cannot but do, you must acknowledge it to be necessary that you should be taken from yourself, and all worldly things, that you might serve your God. But besides,

2.2.2 HE WAS OUR GREATEST EXAMPLE OF SELF-DENIAL

We cannot reasonably look upon him as a hard master, who submitted himself to that which he has imposed upon us, being himself the greatest example of self-denial and forsaking all that ever was. What do you think of his appearing in our frail flesh, of his low estate in the world, of his pain and travail, of this thorny crown and cross? Was there not self-denial in all this, and such as angels and men may justly wonder and be astonished at for ever?

> *He, who being in the form of God, thought it no robbery to be equal with God, made himself of no reputation, and took upon him the form of a servant, and was made in the likeness of a man, and being found in fashion as a man, humbled himself and became obedient unto death, even the death of the cross.* (Philippians 2:6-8)

He, who might have commanded all the riches and glory of the world, as being Lord of all, *'became poor, that by his poverty we might be made rich'* (2 Corinthians 8:9). He, who made all mankind to serve and please him, *'pleased not himself'*, but

*He could not be the author of salvation to us
without taking away that which was our ruin
and destruction.*

became a servant for our good (Romans 15:3). He who could have had more than *'twelve Legions of angels for his guard'* (Matthew 26:53), yielded his cheeks to be smitten, his face to be spat upon, his back to be scourged, his hands and feet to be nailed to an infamous tree, and his side and heart to be pierced by the vilest sinners, whom with one word of his mouth he might have turned into hell.

Thus did our great and good Master deny himself and forsake all. And can we poor worthless wretches think it much to deny our vile selves, and to forsake those little things which we call our own, for his sake, and in obedience to his command? Had he dealt with us as those that once sat in Moses' chair did with their disciples, *'laying heavy burdens upon them, and grievous to be borne, which they themselves would not touch with one of their fingers'* (Matthew 23:4), we might have had some seeming cause of complaint. But since he himself has borne the burden which he has laid upon us, yes, and far more, we are most unreasonable people if we open our mouths against him. He is too soft and delicate a servant that would fare better than his Lord and be exempted from that work which his Lord disdains not to put his hand unto.

2.2.3 HE HAS MADE US FOR HIMSELF

I beseech you, friend, tell me what it is which you judge hard and unreasonable in this commandment. Is it that we should believe ourselves to be what we really are, and that we should demean ourselves in the world accordingly? Is it that we who are as nothing ourselves, and have nothing ourselves, and should be as nothing to ourselves, should be in subordination to him of whom we *are*, and from whom we have received *all*? Is it that he who has made us for himself, and who has freely given us all we do possess, will dispose of us and all according to his pleasure? Is it that we should prefer him before ourselves and his will before our own, and be ready and willing to part with all that he has given us, whenever he is pleased to call for it?

Is it that we should be content to receive difficulty from him as well as good, when he shall see it fit for his own glory and our greater good? I dare say that there is nothing in all this that you may fairly object to – and this is all that is required of you. But yet further,

2.2.4 WHAT HE REQUIRES IS ADVANTAGEOUS TO US

Suppose it appear after all that what is here required is not only just and reasonable, but hugely profitable and advantageous for us. May we not justly look upon those who quarrel with it to be very unreasonable? And truly thus it is, and thus it will appear to be, upon very little consideration. It is no small advantage to be at liberty to obey God entirely and to be able to do it with ease, with delight and pleasure. It is no little benefit to be out of the reach of the devil's malice and of all those dangerous weapons wherewith he assaults and destroys poor souls.

And this we shall infallibly obtain by the practice and performance of this one duty. For what is it that indisposes us to the service of God, that makes his righteous and holy laws to be grievous and uneasy to us, but our believing we are something by ourselves, and choosing to dispose of ourselves according to our own wills?

What is it that gives the devil so much advantage over us but our disorderly passions and affections? And whence have all his temptations their force and power, and all his artifices their success, but from our inordinate love of ourselves and these worldly things? And therefore when we have put off this love, and banished these things from our hearts as we are taught to do, we have disarmed our enemy, or taken off the edge of all his weapons. We have baffled his accursed policies and secured ourselves from his devices. To those that are dead, people may talk of riches and honours and fleshly pleasures as long as they please; they may threaten them with reproaches and pains, and other evil things, till they have wearied themselves, and not find them moved in the least. And no less unmoveable shall we be, to all the temptations of the devil, if we are but perfectly dead to them.

These are great advantages but there is yet one more, no less considerable in the esteem of some, namely, that this will raise us up above all the troubles, perplexities and sorrows of this miserable world. Let what will come upon us here, it shall never be able to hurt us. For whence have all the evil things of the world (as we are wont to call them) their sting and edge, but from our unrenounced selves, our unkilled lusts and passions? We will be something! We will do everything! And everything must be as we will have it! But in the event we find we are nothing, and that we can do nothing, and when the stubborn things will not comply with us – then we are troubled, we are in pain, we are overwhelmed with grief and sorrow. This is an evil that has no remedy but self-denial and resignation to God – and this is a remedy that never fails. When we have put off ourselves as we ought, and disengaged our affections from all earthly things, and can give God leave to dispose of his own creatures, and to govern his own world, then we shall be in peace, then we shall be happy – and not till then. Then nothing can go against us because we shall be willing to comply with everything.

By this time I hope I have perfectly reconciled you to this duty, and that you are resolved to put it in practice. It remains now that I show you as briefly as may be how to do it. And,

2.3 YOU HAVE BEEN ACCUSTOMED TO SERVE YOURSELF

Because you will certainly meet with many and great difficulties in your first endeavours, and the difficulties will be the more and the greater, the more you have loved yourself and the world, and have been accustomed to please yourself and to indulge your affections, it will be necessary. . .

2.3.1 YOU WILL MEET WITH MANY AND GREAT DIFFICULTIES

That you enter upon the practice of it with the strongest convictions possible, both of the necessity and reasonableness of it. And that you arm yourself with such considerations as may beat down all opposition, and effectually encourage you against all the difficulties you can encounter. To this purpose you may make use of all that I have already said, and of many other things which my design will not permit me to give an account of. And after this manner may you discourse with your own heart concerning it. I am told that if I will be a true Christian I must deny myself and forsake the world, and take up my cross. I am told it by Christ himself, and if I do not believe him, why do I call him my Lord, and profess to trust in him as my Saviour? I know that his words have been confirmed and are confirmed daily by a thousand instances. Indeed, I myself am an unhappy instance of the truth of them, having made but little progress in Christian knowledge, and less in Christian virtue, merely for want of a serious regard for them. But if I do believe them, why do I not practise them accordingly?

Does not my everlasting happiness depend upon my being a Christian? Indeed, can I reasonably stick at anything that is needful for the securing myself of that? Is it fit that such a poor derivative thing as I am should take it upon myself to be absolute and independent? What have I done for myself heretofore, and what can I do for myself hereafter, that I should presume to please myself or seek myself in anything? I cannot add one inch to my stature, I cannot make one hair white or black, I cannot do myself the least good, nor remove from myself the lightest evil. And shall I take upon me to do my own will without respect to him, by whom alone I am, and without whose influence and blessing I can do nothing? And what is the world that I should set my heart upon it, and prefer it before my God and Saviour? Did my love of it ever do me any good? Or will it do me any without God's blessing? Or when I am to leave it that I should cleave at present so close unto it? I know that it is God alone that gives me any portion in it, that gives me any comfort by it, and I know that he can deprive me of both when he pleases.

And therefore I shall be not only a rebel but a fool if I don't resign myself and the world to him, and say, 'Whatever is laid upon me, it is the Lord, let him do whatsoever seems good unto him.'

Come therefore, O my heart, let us be no longer rebels against heaven, and enemies to our own happiness. We are not our own, we are not the world's, but we are God's, we are Christ's, and therefore let God dispose of us as he will, and let him give those worldly things to whom he pleases, so that we may have his favour and enjoy it for ever.

O naughty self! How do I detest you for taking so much upon you, as you have done hitherto. O vain, O transitory world! I abhor you, I renounce you utterly. Court me no more with your foolish pleasures, with your glittering bravery, with your deceitful shows. I am now dying and I will be for ever dead unto you, that I may follow Christ, and live unto my God.

Favour these good desires, favour them with your grace, O my God, and suffer not a soul that earnestly aspires towards you to fall short of you.

With these and such like thoughts, you will do well to enter upon the practice of this duty. But then, I advise you,

2.3.2 BEGIN EVERY DAY WITH THESE THOUGHTS

To do as much as you can to keep these and the like thoughts continually in your mind. However, fail not to begin every day with them. When you first behold the light in the morning, after you have sent up your heart to God in some short acknowledgements of his mercy towards you, tell your heart that you have by God's goodness another day added to your life, which you must employ for him and his service. He has bestowed it on you, and not for the pleasing of yourself and the satisfying of your lusts. Charge your heart, as it will answer for it at the great day, that it take care to do so consistently. Like thoughts and resolutions will do well again about noon and indeed, at any time of the day, and the oftener they return into your mind, the more easily and speedily will you come to that perfect resignation which you are concerned to aim at. But yet further,

2.3.3 EXERCISES OF MORTIFICATION AND SELF-DENIAL

It will behoove you to be frequent in exercises of mortification and self-denial. Refrain your wonted liberties, and deny yourself your accustomed satisfactions. Acquaint yourself sometimes with hardships, and turn not always away from sufferings, remembering that you are a soldier under the ensign of the cross, and therefore must not be nice and tender, soft and delicate. Mortify your senses, and accustom them to those things that are least agreeable, knowing that there are some offices to be done sometimes by a Christian, such as visiting poor prisoners, and dressing of poor people's sores. Which people of a nice and squeamish sense will hardly be persuaded to perform.

Mortify your passions likewise, and keep them strictly within their bounds. For as he is a beast that is a slave to sense, so is he a fool that is governed by his passions. In one word, consider yourself well, mark your temper, your inclinations and affections, and keep yourself and them under constant discipline and correction. Have you a trifling wanton spirit? Are you much delighted with the ridicule, banter, jokes and jestings of wanton fancies and loose tongues? Fail not, I beseech you, to restrain your inclinations. Avoid the company of light and vain persons, and turn away your thoughts from trivial matters, to the concernment of a soul that must shortly appear before the bar of a just and holy God, remembering that the Master whom you profess to serve was a serious, grave and useful person, and not a buffoon or stage player. It was the grief of a devout man many years ago (St Bernard) to observe the lightness, laughter and security of many Christians, and his continual fear that he should see them forsaken of the divine grace of which they showed themselves to be unmindful.

What grief, what fear, do you think would have possessed his heart if he had lived in this age and had been a witness of our vanity of this kind? We live in a merry world at present, and nothing is sacred or weighty enough to escape our jokes. But believe it, God will shortly spoil our vain mirth, and make us serious whether we will or not.

Are you soft and slothful, inclined to sensuality and voluptuousness? Rouse up yourself, and be always doing. Take up with plain food, fast often, lie on a hard bed, go frequently to the house of mourning, and keep him continually in your eye, who, after a life of continued travail in doing good, had no easier a bed than a cross to rest upon. Do the riches of the world please you? Refuse them when they are offered, or let the hand of liberality immediately distribute them to those that want them. And keep in mind those good individuals, whom your Bible tells you of, who, though they could have enriched themselves by miracles, yet continued poor, and had not so much as a house to put their heads in. Do worldly honours tickle you, and the applause of others delight you?

Retire from public offices, and hide yourself in the meanness and obscurity of a country life. Be exact and open in the practice of those virtues which are most unfashionable and which the generality of people have a mean opinion of. Forget not that there was a person once in the world who was able to have governed the whole world, and that led the greatest part of his life in the country villages and among poor people, and would not have his great and mighty works be publicly spoken of.

This is to practise self-denial, and by these and like practices you will in a short time arrive at that perfect resignation to which I desire to lead you. But then in the last place,

2.3.4 BE EMPLOYED NOT FOR YOURSELF BUT FOR GOD

Be sure that in these practices and in whatever else you do, you take nothing to yourself; but refer yourself and all to almighty God. You may begin well, my friend, in renouncing yourself. Yet you may end ill in that very self which you did at first renounce. If you do these things for the satisfaction of yourself, and seek your own glory in them. Forget not therefore this last advice: 'It is not for yourself but for God that you must be employed, if you wish to be entirely resigned to God and be forever united with God. You must be as nothing to yourself, and the world must be as nothing to you, that God may be all in all.

CHAPTER
3
==

TO GIVE OURSELVES TO GOD

3.1 *Containing a third advice to give up ourselves souls and bodies entirely to God, with several arguments to persuade us to it.*

3.2 *Containing several directions how to put into practice this advice of giving ourselves to God.*

3.1 GIVE UP OUR SOULS AND BODIES ENTIRELY TO GOD

 IVE UP YOURSELF, your soul and body, all the faculties of the one, and all the members of the other, together with all you have in the world, wholly and entirely to God through Christ Jesus, uniting yourself to him in the closest manner, and by the strongest bonds that possibly you can, resolve to be his, and only his for ever. To make you capable of doing this was the design of my former advice, and if you can practise that well, you will readily follow this. For by breaking those bonds which kept you from God, you will as naturally rise to him as fire ascends upwards, when that which depresses it or keeps it down is removed from it. And therefore, fewer words may serve to enforce this advice upon you. The heads of some few considerations I shall briefly offer you. Enlarge upon them as you see good. In the first place then,

3.1.1 WE ARE GOD'S CREATURES

You must and do acknowledge yourself to be God's creature. He is the only spring and root of your being and life. And is it not just then that you should be and live to him and to him alone? Are you not a very unreasonable creature if you refuse to be his, by whom alone you are, and without whom you cannot be at all? Yes surely.

3.1.2 GOD IS OUR ONLY SUPPORTER

You must acknowledge God to be the only supporter, preserver and maintainer of your life and being. You live by him as surely as the tree by its root, and if he withdraw his quickening influence and power but one moment, you are dead without remedy. Those necessities for the preserving of life which the world furnishes you with are all fallen from him. And all the virtue and efficacy they have for that purpose are no less from him. It is he that refreshes you by heat and light, that nourishes you by meat and drink, that cures you by medicine and cleansing, and without him you could have no nourishment, no health, no refreshment. And with what reason, then, can you withhold yourself from him? Surely with none at all.

3.1.3 GOD IS OUR SAVIOUR

You believe God to be your Saviour, i.e. that he has given you his only begotten Son to deliver you from sin and death, and to bring you to everlasting life. And that as he, as a man, offered up himself a sacrifice upon the cross for your sins, so he has undertaken to bring back your erring and lost soul to God. And therefore you are a most unworthy and ungrateful wretch if you will not comply with his gracious undertaking, but refuse to be Christ's, that you may be God's for ever.

3.1.4 HIS HOLY SPIRIT IS WORKING IN YOU

You do believe and acknowledge that for this end he has taken possession of you by his Holy Spirit, who is continually working in you, to help you by putting off yourself, and all selfish inclinations and desires, and by abandoning all that is dear to you. This is to offer up yourself, as Abraham offered up his Isaac, a sacrifice unto God. And therefore you cannot, without the guilt of the most abominable sacrifice, take upon you to be anything – or to do anything – but for God and to God. See 1 Corinthians 6:19-20.

3.1.5 AT YOUR BAPTISM YOU ARE JOINED TO GOD

You have made a show, an outward profession of giving up yourself to God, and of being God's, long ago. This you did at your baptism, when renouncing the devil, the world and the flesh, you did give up your self to God the Father, Son and Holy Ghost. And this profession you have (probably) renewed often at the table of the Lord, where commemorating and giving thanks to God for the greatest expression of the greatest love to man that ever was, you did 'offer and present yourself, your soul and body to be a reasonable, holy and living sacrifice to the Lord'. And you have seemed to the world to this very day to accept all this. And therefore, if you will not be God's after all this, by the full consent of your heart, then you are the falsest and vilest hypocrite upon earth, and an accursed traitor to your great Creator, to your gracious and loving Saviour. To all this you may add,

3.1.6 FAITHFUL SERVICE AND OBEDIENCE FOR EVER

This is that holiness which the Scriptures so frequently recommend unto you, and without which you cannot hope to see the Lord. When things are separated from common uses and are given up to God so as never to be made use of but for him, or in his worship and service, they are called holy things. And so indeed they are, so far as things can be. Thus, when you have separated yourself, taken off your heart from all created things and have given up yourself to God, to be his and only his – in faithful service and obedience for ever – you are holy, and not till then. And if you think otherwise, you do dangerously deceive yourself. Add to this,

3.1.7 RESIGN YOURSELF TO GOD

This is your perfection, and the greatest perfection you are capable of. You can do nothing better than to resign yourself to God. And you cannot possibly be in any better state than in a state of pure resignation to him. And therefore in the last place,

3.1.8 HOLINESS, PERFECTION AND HAPPINESS ARE THE SAME

You may safely believe that this is your happiness, and the greatest happiness you can attain unto. The truth is, these three words, holiness, perfection and happiness, though they differ in sound, are all the very same in sense and signification. He that says that the saints in heaven are blessed, says no other thing than this, that they are made perfect. And he that says that they are made perfect, says no other thing than this, that they are fully and completely holy. And he that speaks this says no more than that they are entirely God's, that they are perfectly disengaged from everything that might withhold them in the least from him. They are so united to him that nothing can separate or dissolve the union. All that I would now persuade you to is but to make yourself as perfect and happy as you can be. And I think in this case it should be no hard matter to prevail with you when you cannot but see your interest in that which is recommended to you as your duty. It is not impossible, if you are the person I now suppose you to be, but you must yield your full consent to it. And therefore I leave these things to your serious thoughts, and proceed to give you some directions on how to perform this good and happy work.

3.2 DIRECTIONS FOR THE HOLY LIFE

That you are concerned to take the greatest care to do it well, I presume I need not tell you. And therefore, as I do earnestly recommend the following directions to you, so I hope you will not fail to practise them. And because it is a matter of great moment in everything to begin well, I advise you,

3.2.1 SEPARATE YOURSELF FROM THE WORLD

Separate yourself for some time from the world. Retire into your closet, or into some secret place, where no eye may see you, and nothing divert or disturb you. And when you are there, consider that you are there about a business of the greatest importance to you. You are to give yourself to God, to unite yourself most firmly to him. But of yourself, and without God's special grace, you are not able to do it. If he does not draw you, if he does not overcome your sorry heart by the sweet and powerful influences of his love, you will make but faint and feigned offers of yourself unto him. And therefore you must not fail in the first place,

3.2.1.1 Talk with God alone

To fall upon your senses, and with the greatest reverence and submission, to acquaint him with the desires of your soul, and to beg his favourable acceptance of them and his blessing upon them. And if you don't know how to do it better, you may make use of this form of words:

> My Lord and my God, you know the very bottom of my heart, and my desires are not hidden from you. I am encouraged by my own happy experience of your goodness, as well as by your gracious declaration of your will, to present myself before you, even though I know myself to be unworthy of the least favour from you. I am ashamed when I think how I have demeaned myself towards you, and that I have lived so long a stranger. I have even been an enemy to you, taking upon me to rule myself, and to run myself in the main course of my life without the least regard to you. I abhor myself for it, and acknowledge that I deserve for ever to be abandoned by you.
>
> But you have not dealt with me according to my deserts – blessed be your goodness for it! And therefore I now desire without hesitation to return unto you, and renounce all interest and propriety in myself. I detest all my former ungodly practices. I

desire to give up myself wholly and entirely to you.

I would be yours, and only yours, in all love and service, in perfect submission and obedience for ever. But I know I am nothing, and can do nothing of myself. If ever I am yours, as I desire to be, I must be indebted wholly to your goodness for it.

O my God, my Saviour and my sanctifier, turn not your face away from a poor soul that seeks you and places all confidence and comfort in you. But as you have kindled these good desires in my heart, so favour them with your blessing, and confirm, increase and sanctify them.

Reject not that poor gift, which I would make of myself unto you, and enable me to make it in such a manner that it may be pleasing and acceptable in your sight. Lord, hear me, help me and show mercy to me, for Christ Jesus' sake. Amen.

When you have thus offered your desires to God, rise from your knees, and either walking or sitting, as you think best,

3.2.1.2 STIR YOURSELF TO PERFECT SURRENDER

Begin to excite and stir up your soul to a perfect surrender of itself, by the arguments before laid down, pressing them upon yourself with all your might. And that they may have as great an influence upon you as is possible, you may imagine that you hear almighty God speaking to you from heaven in this manner: 'Consider yourself, O creature, and take notice what you are and what good things you do possess; look upon your body and all its useful members. Consider your soul and all its faculties and powers, and observe their several motions and operations, and tell me whence you are and to whom you are indebted for them. Look upon the world that furnishes you with all things necessary and fitting for you, and tell me who was the framer of it, and who made it useful and serviceable to you.'

'Can you deny that I have done all this? And wherefore, then, have you lifted up yourself against me and presumed to act as if you had no dependence upon me or obligation to me? If you sow your seed in your field, you expect to reap the crop. If you did nourish and provide for a poor beast, you think that you may use him at your pleasure. If you make an instrument to work, you have a right to use it. But I have maintained and preserved a creature (hear and be ashamed of yourself) and you will allow me no right and title to him and his service. Tell me, O you unjust and ungrateful wretch, did I ever give you liberty to rule yourself? Did I ever give you occasion to think that I made no reckoning of you or that I expected no acknowledgement from you? No, wretched creature, you knew that I made you for myself and that I would not give away my interest in you. I put a great value upon you, and as I made you capable of serving me, so I expected and desired it from you. Therefore did I love you from the beginning and bestowed innumerable gifts upon you. I gave you all things that were fitting for you and assured you that I would withhold no good thing from you. Yes, I gave you myself in my only begotten Son, who descended out of my bosom to assure you of my love, as well as to convince you that you had deserved my hatred.

'You can rage against a poor employee that neglects your business and seems to slight you. Your poor neighbour, who has no dependence upon you, feels the effects of your displeasure if he chance to wrong you. They must seek your pardon and crouch before you, and think themselves beholden to you, if by so doing they can make their peace. And yet I have humbled myself to you, you vile worm, and have not spared my own Son that I might spare you and bring you to a due sense of your duty to me. Heaven and earth can witness for me that I have stooped low enough in desiring the friendship of rebellious dust and ashes. And others shall witness the justice of my severity to you, if so much love and condescension will not work upon you.'

Here you may pause a while and observe how your soul is affected with these things. And then you may imagine again that you hear almighty God speaking further to you and more fully relating the wonderful history of his love in Christ Jesus.

And after he has given you an account of his mean birth, of his humble and painful life, of his bloody and cruel death, and his design and end in all this, proceeding to show you with how much love and with what tender regard for you he left this world and ascended to his Father. And how, that after he had done and suffered in his own person, as much as was necessary and fitting for him, he sent the Holy Ghost to complete the great and good work of your eternal salvation. And then imagine that he tells you what that blessed and Holy Spirit has for his part done for you, what gifts he has bestowed, what wonders he has wrought, what arts and methods he has used, and with what goodness and patience, and long-suffering, to bring you to a right understanding and a real sense of all his love and all your duty to him. All this to excite, encourage and enable you to the performance of it.

And in the end he speaks to you in this manner: 'Wretch that you are, must all this love be lost upon you? And must I love you for ever, after all that I have done for you? Will nothing work upon your hard heart, upon your proud and stubborn will? Will nothing conquer the perverseness of your spirit? Not the commands of your maker, nor the death of your Saviour, nor the good motions and inspirations of your sanctifier?

'Can you withstand my power, that you are thus obstinate against my goodness? And if you will allow me to save you, do you think that I am not able to destroy you? O foolish creature and unwise! Consider these thing seriously, and as you ought. Remember what you have done, and what unreasonable courses you have taken, and proceed no further in your folly. Return to that love that calls you, that entreats you, that would save you.'

Here you may pause a little. If anything more is necessary to shame and humble you, to soften and melt you, you may turn yourself to consider your own engagements, and to charge yourself with that monstrous foolishness which you have, and will continue to be guilty of, if you now withstand the calls of God. And that your foolishness may appear the more detestable, you may consider finally this: that which you are now called to do is not anything unjust, dishonest or unreasonable. It is not to destroy yourself, or to make yourself miserable, but on the contrary, it is to do the most just, the most reasonable and the best thing that you are capable of doing. It is to return to the author of your being, and thereby serve the end of your creation. It is the only happiness and rest of your soul. It is to unite yourself to the supreme good, to make yourself his, and to make him yours, for ever. And is this a thing so repugnant to you that you need so much invitation and persuasion to accept it? O my soul! My foolish soul, may you say, what can you say for yourself in this case? Is there any excuse for your folly? Any plea for your wickedness? No, far be it from you to seek for any. Let us rather amend what we have done amiss, and be more wise for the time to come.

We would have been happy if we had needed as much of an invitation to destroy ourselves. But since we could do that with very little or none at all, let us no longer withstand this which is so earnest and begs us to save ourselves. In turning yourself to God (in whose presence you have been all this while) you may speak (as I hope you will be able with truth to do) in this manner to him:

'I am overcome, I am overcome, O God. I can no longer withstand your almighty love. I must and I do yield myself a captive to it. I am yours. I do acknowledge this by all right, and I will be yours for ever, by the full consent of my heart.

'I can do no less in return for that wonderful love you have shown me, and I can do no more. O, let this little that I can do be accepted by you, and receive me for your own. Take possession of me by your Spirit, and let it preserve me for ever to yourself, according as I do now sincerely resign myself, and all I have, to you.'

3.2.1.3 GIVE YOURSELF BODY AND SOUL TO GOD

Casting yourself upon the ground, say thus, and say it with all your heart and soul.

'To God the Father, Son and Holy Ghost, my creator, redeemer and sanctifier, do I give myself soul and body, and all that belongs unto me, to be guided, governed and disposed of according to his will, and to his honour and glory, and may he be a witness to this my act, which I promise never to revoke. And may I never obtain the least favour from him if I do it not with an upright heart, and a sure purpose to make it good to my life's end. You are my witness, O my God, and so be also my helper with your continued grace, that I shall be faithful to you according to my heart's desire. Amen, Amen.'

3.2.1.4 MAKE A PRIVATE VOW BETWEEN YOURSELF AND YOUR MAKER

But then as in matters of the world, that which is done in private between one person and another, must in some cases receive a further confirmation by such solemnities as are appointed by human laws. Thus that which you have done between God and your own soul must be further confirmed, and completed, by those solemnities which the laws of God require. Therefore fail not to take the first opportunity that is offered you to go to the table of the Lord. And having prepared yourself at home by such meditations as I have before taught you, and by reading some good book of the holy sacrament (such as Dr Patrick's *Christian Sacrifice*, which I desire may find a place both in your closet and in your heart) renew there what you have done in private, and in public avow it and confirm it. At that holy table God will not fail to meet you attended with an innumerable company of holy angels, and he strictly requires and expects it from you.

Therefore, when you are at that table, and behold what manner of love is there showed you, and which cannot but draw your very heart from you, remember what you are to do, and let your heart speak in this manner to almighty God:

'There is all the reason in the world, O heavenly Father, that I should give up myself entirely to you, since you have not withheld your Son, your only Son from me. There is all the reason in the world, O my blessed Saviour, that I should surrender myself, and all I have, into your hands, since you did offer yourself a sacrifice upon the cross for me, and do now offer these holy pledges of the all-sufficient virtue of that sacrifice to me. There is all the reason in the world that I should resign myself to you, O holy and blessed Spirit, since you do offer yourself to be a principle of holiness and life in me.

'And therefore, I do now accept with all thankfulness those great and inestimable favours, and do declare my acceptance of them in the sight of these your servants, and all your holy angels here present, by receiving those tokens and pledges of them according to your command and institution. I give up myself and all I have to you, and declare it before the face of all these witnesses, and I earnestly desire that even my unworthy self may be accepted through this my poor gift, the perfect sacrifice and oblation of my dearest Saviour. May it be sanctified by

*"Whom have I in heaven but you? And there is
none upon earth
that I desire besides you"* (Psalm 73:25)

the Holy Ghost, and be owned by my God, to the everlasting praise of the holy, blessed and undivided Trinity, whose I am and whose I will be for ever and ever. *Amen, Amen.*'

3.2.1.5 SURRENDER YOURSELF ALONE AND IN WRITING

When you are gone from this holy table, retire as soon as possibly you can, and while these good thoughts are warm in your breast, into your closet and there take the book of your spiritual accounts into your hand (for I would not have you to be without such a book, for recording these things wherein the welfare of your soul is greatly concerned) and with your pen write thus:

'In such a year and such a month, and on such a day, I did through God's grace, with all the devotion of my heart and soul, make an entire surrender of myself, and all things belonging to me, to almighty God proclaiming and vowing that he should have the full guiding, governing and disposing of me and mine for ever.'

And then, that you may have a more distinct understanding of what you have done, and what you are obliged to do for the time to come, you may underwrite these following particulars, namely,

'I have given myself up entirely to God and therefore I must not serve myself, but him all the days of my life.

'I have given him my understanding: and therefore my chief care and study must be to know him, his nature, his perfections, his works, his will. These must be the subject of my meditations night and day; as for all other things, they must be as dross and dung to me; *"and the knowledge of them must be as loss for the excellency of the knowledge of God in Christ"* (Philippians 3:8). I must believe all his revelations, and silencing all the carnal reasonings against whatsoever he teaches me, I must rest myself on his veracity, being fully persuaded that he can neither be deceived himself, nor deceive me. (See Romans 4:19-20.)

'I have given him my will, and therefore I must have no will of my own. Whatever he wills, I must will also. I must will his glory in all things, as he does, and that must be my chief end in everything. I must prefer it before all desirable things, and subordinate my own desires, delights and satisfactions to it. I must say, as the Psalmist did, *"Whom have I in heaven but you? And there is none upon earth, that I desire besides you"* (Psalm 73:25). I must do whatsoever God commands me and forbear whatever he forbids, and I must do it for this reason: because he does command or forbid me. Indeed, *"I must delight to do it"* (Psalm 40:8). And it must be to me *"as my meat and drink"* (John 4:34). I must be content to suffer whatever he will lay upon me, and though it may be his pleasure to lay hard things upon me, and grievous to be borne, yet I must not complain or murmur. But with cheerfulness, alacrity and thankfulness, I will submit myself to it. Whatever threatens me, I must say, *"It is the Lord, let him do what seems good to him"* (1 Samuel 3:18), and whatever befalls me, *"I must give thanks, for that is his will concerning me in Christ Jesus"* (1 Thessalonians 5:18).

'I have given him all the passions and affections of my soul and therefore he must direct them, govern and set bounds for them. He must have my love, my fear, my delight, my joy – and nothing in the world must have any share in these or any other of my affections. What he loves, I must love. What he hates, I must hate. What he is well pleased with, I must rejoice in. What he is grieved with, I must mourn for. The objects of his pity I must have compassion on, and those of his wrath and indignation I must be zealous against. And all in such measures only to the degree he is pleased to allow me.

'I have given him my body, and therefore must glorify him

with it. I must not dare to abuse it by gluttony, drunkenness, adultery, fornication or any other uncleanness. I must look upon it as his temple, and therefore must preserve it pure and holy, fit for my God to dwell in (see 1 Corinthians 6:19). I must not wrong it by pampering or indulging it, nor by neglecting it, nor by showing too much rigour towards it in overmuch fasting, watching, labouring, etcetera. But I must keep my body, as far as in me lies, healthy, vigorous, active and fit to do him all manner of service that he shall call for.

'I have given him my senses, my eyes, my ears and so forth. And therefore, they must be always open to good, but to evil, and all the occasions of it, they must be shut.

'I have given him all my members, and therefore they must be no longer instruments of unrighteousness unto sin (Romans 6:13) but instruments of righteousness unto God. My tongue must show forth his praise, my hands must do his works, and my foot must carry me with speed unto it.

'I have given him not myself only, but also all that belongs to me, and therefore my children, my friends, my employees must all be his, if I can make them so.

'I have given him all my worldly goods. And therefore I must prize them and use them only for him. His house, his priests, his poor must have their portions from me with a willing mind. And though I have no more than necessaries for my life, yet I must be content to part with them, when my Lord shall need them, or command me to resign them.

'I have given him my credit and reputation. Therefore I must value it, and endeavour to maintain it only in respect to him, as it may do him service, and advance his honour in the world.

'I have given him myself and all. Therefore I must look upon myself to be nothing and to have nothing outside of him. He must be the sole disposer, governor and guider of myself and all. He must be my portion and my all.'

And then, in the close you may add this.

'Thus have I given myself to God, and to all this have I bound myself in the most solemn manner. With my own hand do I now testify my full consent to it, and I am resolved to make good the whole and every part of it, God assisting me, to my life's end. I doubt not but I shall meet with many temptations to the contrary. I shall be often told of my singularity and preciseness, and some may tell me in kindness that I do more than is necessary, and that I must accommodate or fit myself to this or that person, company, thing, custom, etcetera. But my answer shall be to all, I am not my own, I am not for myself, nor for my friends, nor for the world, nor for its customs, but for my God. I will give to Caesar what I owe to Caesar, and to God what I owe to God. The Lord be merciful to me, his unworthy servant.'

All this I say you will do well to write in your book of spiritual accounts. But if you cannot write, fail not to fix it in your memory, and as often as you are called to the table of the Lord, take a view of it, or repeat it to yourself, and call yourself strictly to account how you have made it good, and how and wherein you have failed. Give God thanks for what you have been able to do, and humble yourself before him for all that you have omitted, confessing it with sorrow, and earnestly begging pardon for it, renewing your resolutions and vows, and imploring a greater measure of his grace to enable you to do better for the time to come.

But did I say that you must do this as often as you are called to the table of the Lord? I must tell you that you should do it more often. You should do it once a week at least, Saturday in the evening or early in the morning on the Lord's day. For so often at least were the primitive Christians wont to receive the holy sacrament, and that we do it not as often as they did is not for our praise or commendation. Indeed to put off this till our usual times of communion is to put it off to a time when we can hardly do it well. Because many things will be forgotten by us, or else we shall be overwhelmed with too great a multitude.

There is not one but will find work enough at the end of one week, to call to mind how his heart has been disposed, his tongue employed, and what good or evil deeds he has done, with the several circumstances belonging to them, during that time; and how imperfect an account of these things, then, can they give to themselves, and to almighty God, who are to look back a full quarter of a year and to call all their ways to remembrance?

Let this therefore be done, I pray you, at least as often as I have said, and if you cannot be so happy as to take communion weekly, then this will in some measure supply the want of it, and put you into a better disposition to give yourself to God when you do take holy communion, and it will unite yourself more firmly to him. I must confess I am not able to promise you, but you will discern many failings when you come thus to examine yourself, though you have been ever so careful to keep close to God and to demean yourself as God's. Let not this discourage you in the least, because you have to do with a God that knows your frailty, and abounds in mercy and compassion towards you. And as long as you do not withdraw your heart from him, nor slack your endeavours to make good your resolutions and vows, you may rest yourself assured that you shall not want the choicest tokens of his love, a daily supply of grace and strength to obey and please him. You may feel yourself at first to be weak as a child, but be not dismayed at it for you will find that in a little time the spirit which first breathed into you this new life will preserve and cherish it, and make you to *grow up to a perfect man, unto the measure of the stature of the fullness of Christ*' (Ephesians 4:13).

Thus have I shown you (my dear friend), how you may become a real Christian, i.e. in the language of the Scripture, *'a new creature in Christ Jesus'* (2 Corinthians 5:17). And let me tell you for your comfort, that when these things are done, you may safely account yourself to be one. And all those privileges which the holy Scriptures assure you do belong to real Christians, you may justly claim as belonging to yourself. Are they one with Christ? So are you. Have they the spirit of Christ? So have you. Have they the fellowship with the Father and the Son? So have you. Are they the children of God, heirs of God, and co-heirs with Christ? So are you.

This is a happy and honourable estate. No ambitious soul can aim at anything higher, no heart can desire anything better. It is that to which all that call themselves Christians do pretend but they, and they only, that have thus resigned themselves to God, have attained to it.

But now I must tell you that by how much greater your happiness is in this estate, by that much more you must be concerned to take care that you fall not away from it. Use all diligence to keep yourself in a firm possession of it, remembering that you are not yet in heaven where there is no falling away from God, but in a place of many temptations, where many do draw back, and after they have known the way of righteousness, do turn from it (1 Peter 2:21). For this purpose I must proceed to give you some further directions, but contracting my thoughts as much as may be, that I may not burden you with too big a book.

*You must endeavour daily to grow in the knowledge of God,
and to get more clear, distinct, firm, well-settled
apprehensions of the things of God.*

CHAPTER
4

GROW IN THE KNOWLEDGE OF GOD

4.1 *Containing the fourth advice, To grow in the knowledge of God and of the things of God.*

4.2 *Containing several directions how to improve in all divine knowledge.*

4.1 GROW DAILY IN GOD

OU MUST ENDEAVOUR daily to grow in the knowledge of God, and to get more clear, distinct, firm, well-settled apprehensions of the things of God. The reason for this advice is very plain, namely, that the more you know of God, and the more clear your apprehensions of divine things are, the better you will love God and the more closely will your heart cleave unto him. There are some things indeed of such a nature that the less men know them, the more they esteem and love them while they look upon them at a distance, and know them but imperfectly. They seem great and good, worthy of their esteem and love, but when they come to handle them, and know them thoroughly, they are convinced that they are neither.

But now the things of God are of another sort. Such is the perfection of their nature, that the more they are unfolded to us, the more we admire them, and the more strongly do they draw our souls towards them. And if there be any people that do not value them, or are not in love with them, we may be confident that they do not know them. Is it I that speak this? Or does not the Scripture also speak the same? Why then does it so often tell us of wicked men, *'That they know not God, that they know not the way of the Lord, nor the judgements of their God'* (Jeremiah 5:4; 9:4)? And what is it that St John means when he tells us, *'That by this we know that we know him, if we keep his commandments: he that says he knows him, and keeps not his commandments, is a liar, and the truth is not in him'* (1 John 2:3-4)?

Does not this imply plainly that they who know God truly will obey him, and that the reason why they do not love and obey him is their ignorance of him, or the imperfection of their knowledge? Either they know not God at all, or their knowledge is so weak, so slight, so imperfect, that it makes little or no impression upon their hearts. Their conceptions of God are like those concepts which we have of some things in our sleep, which either affect us not at all, or are forgotten by us as soon as we awake. We believe, and we believe rightly, that the saints in heaven shall never fall from God, but will love and serve him for ever, without the least failing or imperfection. And what is the reason of it? Surely it is because they *'know him as they are known of him'* (1 Corinthians 13:12). Or as St John speaks, *'they see him as he is'* (1 John 3:2), i.e. they have the clearest, firmest, the most full and comprehensive knowledge of him that creatures can have. By this they are transformed into his image and made like unto him. He that does know God truly, does also know himself, and he that does know God and himself truly, cannot but keep himself in a state of resignation and subjection to God continually.

He will feel those impressions upon himself, which holy Job did, when God had made himself a little better known to him than he was before (Job 38:39) and will say from the very bottom of his heart, as holy Job did, *'Behold I am vile'* (40:4), he will know that it is not for a worm to contend with the creator of all things, not for him that was born like a wild ass's colt (as one of Job's friends speaks) to presume to find out the almighty perfectly. He will feel the truth of what the Psalmist says in Psalm 9:10, *'They that know thy name, will put their trust in you'*, and will heartily assent to that saying of a great man, *'that the more we reject ourselves, and commit ourselves to God, the better it is for us'* [Mich. De Montaign]. He will say as a devout man once did, *'What are you O Lord, and what am I?'*

He will be continually admiring his sovereign greatness, and will be no less sensible of his own worthlessness and nothingness. He that knows God truly will also know the world. And he that knows God and the world aright, will never be drawn from God by any of the world's allurements. He will know that the world is nothing in itself. And will he set his heart upon that which is not? He will know that without God, it can contribute no more to his happiness than it did to his being, which he knows himself indebted only to God for. And can that steal away his heart from the author of all good, which never did, nor can, bestow the least good upon him? How vile does this earth seem to us, when we lift up our eyes and look upon the heavens?

Surely much more vile will all things seem to him, whose soul is possessed with a true knowledge of the maker of them. A man once spoke this truth, when being in an ecstasy, and cried out, *'O my God! O my Lord! O the God of my heart! O that all men did know you! They would never offend you, they would ever love you.'* For surely (as the author of the book of Wisdom tells us), *'To know God is perfect righteousness, and to know his power is the root of immortality'* (Wisdom 15:4). This may suffice to show you the reason of my advice. Let me now as briefly, direct you how to practise it.

4.2 DIRECTIONS TO IMPROVE IN DIVINE KNOWLEDGE

4.2.1 LEARN ONLY WHAT IS NECESSARY

To this purpose let me tell you, that you are not concerned to know as much as may be known of God, or as learned men do know, but only so much as is necessary or as may be helpful to keep you entirely resigned and obedient to his will. Therefore you must not trouble yourself with those nice and curious speculations in religion, which are of no use or tendency to this end. That knowledge, whatever the object of it is, which will not conduce to make you better, or prevent your becoming worse than you are, is impertinent, useless and unprofitable. The hunting after it has ruined thousands, but never saved one soul. Those that pursue after it are thus described by St Paul in 1 Timothy 6:3-4 – *'They consent not to wholesome words, and to the doctrine which is according to goodness; they are proud, knowing nothing, but doting about questions and strifes of words.'*

4.2.2 LEARN THE GREAT AND USEFUL THINGS AS WELL AS POSSIBLE

Though you are not concerned to know as much as may be known of God, yet you must endeavour to know these great and useful things I have spoken of as well as possibly you can; and therefore you must not content yourself with that sleight, superficial knowledge which the generality of people have of them, who rather dream of divine things than know them. But you must labour for a clear, distinct apprehension of them, and for a firm and well-grounded persuasion of the truth and goodness of them. And to this purpose you must

4.2.3 APPLY YOURSELF WITH ALL DILIGENCE

Apply yourself to the use of all good means with great care and diligence, remembering that if it be folly to do meaner things slightly (as certainly it is, because many things many times depend upon our least actions), then to be careless and sleight in such a matter as this can be no less than madness. Now the means that you are to use are these that follow:

4.2.3.1 READ THE HOLY SCRIPTURES DAILY

Reading the holy Scriptures, and hearing them read, this you are to do daily; you must borrow some part of every day (to say nothing here of what you are to do upon holy days) from your worldly employments, to read or hear them read. Our blessed Saviour bids us *'Search the scriptures, because in them you think you have eternal life'* (John 5:39). And St Paul tells us, that *'they are able to make us wise unto salvation'* (2 Timothy 3:15). And if any one's words are of greater weight with us than theirs, we ill deserve the name of Christians.

4.2.3.2 READ GOOD BOOKS

I call those books good which treat of the great things of God modestly, discreetly, plainly, convincingly and affectionately: of which sort I know not many in the world, and therefore you are to take the best advice you can find in the choice of them.

4.2.3.3 LISTEN TO SERMONS AND DISCOURSES

Listen to sermons and good discourses made by Christ's ministers, whether in the pulpit upon particular texts of Scripture, or in class, as expositions of some larger portions of it, or of some of the most chief points of religion contained in the catechism. These discourses Christ's ministers are commanded to make for the edification of Christ's Church (see 2 Timothy 4:1-2), and therefore Christian people are bound to attend to them, and they are too wise or too good that have the conceit that they have no need of them. I mean that they are neither wise nor good.

4.2.3.4 CONFER WITH OTHER CHRISTIANS

Frequent conferring with serious Christians about divine things is a means of improving knowledge that has several advantages above any other. In this we instruct others as well as ourselves, imparting our own knowledge to them while we receive of theirs. That which we thus learn, we apprehend more clearly, and are more deeply affected with, than we are with that which we receive any other way. Therefore it is much to be lamented that this is no more used by those that call themselves Christians than we see that it is. And we may infer from the neglect of it that people are not so knowing in the things of God as they believe themselves to be. And I am sure we may conclude from it that they are not so good as they ought to be. They seldom fail to talk of that which they love, when there is occasion offered for it. So also they would never be silent about these things if they had that hearty affection for them which they ought to have.

And as for the common excuse among the more serious sort of people, that they would not be taken for hypocrites (as too many in this last age, among whom this has been in fashion,

*'Search the scriptures, because in them you think
you have eternal life'* (John 5:39).

have discovered themselves to be), it is so far from justifying their neglect that it shows the naughtiness of their hearts: they show themselves more concerned for their own reputation than for the honour of God and for the great concerns of their souls. There would be little or no religion seen in the world if the abuse of it by hypocrites would warrant men to cast off the profession of it. There were too many hypocrites in holy David's time, and *'yet his tongue did not cease to speak of God's righteousness, and of his praise all the day long'* (Psalm 25:28).

And the apostles' times were not so happy as to be without them, and yet they called upon Christians to exhort one another daily (Hebrews 4:13). And to teach and admonish each other, and that by psalms and hymns and spiritual songs, as well as other ways (Colossians 3:16). Those good men thought that the danger of being accounted hypocrites would discharge them from *'seasoning their discourses with salt'*, or from speaking such things in their conversation with each other as might be profitable and minister grace unto the hearers (Ephesians 4:29 and Colossians 6:4). And why we should think that it becomes us to use that unprofitable and corrupt communication which daily proceeds from our mouths without having any respect to the edifying of one another in that which is good? I cannot understand.

4.2.3.5 MEDITATE UPON THE THINGS WE HEAR AND READ

Meditate frequently upon the good things we read and hear. This is another means for the improvement of our knowledge in the things of God, and it is so necessary that without it all the rest will avail us but very little, for this the digesting of what we read and hear. It is that which implants those notices of things which we have got into our heads, in our hearts, and makes them to bring forth those good fruits which in their own nature they are fit to do. It was a good observation of a great man some years ago, that in all human sects there were never any – however peculiar their beliefs – but would in some sort conform their behaviour and square their lives unto it. Whereas this divine and heavenly institution – which we pretend to prefer before all doctrines that ever were in the world – seldom makes Christians serious about our present business. Yet those being in love with their doctrines, however absurd they were, either because they were of their own invention, or because they held their first inventors in great admiration, did so focus their thoughts upon those doctrines that their souls could not but receive such impressions from them – with the consequent effect on their outward behaviour. Whereas most of those that are called Christians, having no such love for this heavenly doctrine, or the author of it, do never focus their thoughts about it – or if they do, it is so seldom, and in so sleight and careless a manner, that it cannot work any good effect upon them.

Did they meditate daily upon it, as holy David did upon God's law (Psalm 119:97)? Did they examine its truth, did they weigh its goodness, did they apply it to themselves, and make trial of its force and power upon their souls? If so, they would be fashioned to the image and likeness of it, and be known by their lives and conversations as different from all other men. You must be frequent then in the use of this meditation, and let no day pass you without spending some time in it. And if you are in such circumstances at any time, that you must either omit to read good books or to meditate, I advise you to omit reading rather than this. For he that reads but little and meditates much will be a wiser and better man than he that reads much and meditates none or but very little.

4.2.3.6 PRAYER

This is a means which must accompany all the rest, and ought never to be omitted, for certain it is that we can know no more of God than we are taught by him. If he does not manifest himself unto us, if he does not enlighten our minds and assist our endeavours, we shall advance but little by all we can do. The Psalmist tells us that it *'is God that teaches men knowledge'* (Psalm 94:10) and St Paul tells us *'That wisdom and knowledge are the gifts of the Spirit'* (1 Corinthians 12:8), and if we desire that Spirit, or those gifts, we must ask for them – for thus did the holy men of old do, as the Scripture assures us (Psalm 25:4; 119:66). And this the apostle St Paul taught us to do when he prayed for the Colossians, *'That they might be filled with the knowledge of God, in all wisdom, and spiritual understanding; That they might walk worthy of the Lord, unto all pleasing, being fruitful in every good work, and increasing in the knowledge of God'* (Colossians 1:9-10). And then in the last place,

4.2.3.7 PRACTISE WHAT WE KNOW

There is another means of improving our knowledge of as great use, though little thought of, as any of the former, namely, the making a right use of that which we know, by applying it to practice and regulating our lives and conversations according to it. By thus using what we know, we shall come to know it better, for there is no knowledge comparable to that which we call experimental and he that tastes *'how good the Lord is, and how good the things of God are'* (Psalm 34:8) knows them as much better than others do, as they that taste the sweetness of honey know it better than they that have only heard of it.

Besides, by this use of what we know, we are put into a

better disposition to know those things which as yet we know not. For, as some of the old heathen wise men were wont to say, *'as no eye can behold the sun, if it has not the image of the sun in it'*, so no man is capable of understanding the things of God, but he whose soul is in some measure fashioned to the likeness of God. And this is confirmed by a more skilful man in divine things than the wisest of them, St Paul, who tells us *'that the natural (or animal) man receives not the things of the Spirit of God, neither can he know them, because they are spiritually discerned'* (1 Corinthians 2:14). This assertion is grounded upon this truth, that there must be some conformity between the knowing faculty, and the thing to be known, or else there can be no knowledge; and therefore, we must improve that little knowledge which we have by the light of nature, according to those small remains of God's image in us, for the mortifying of our naughty corrupt affections. And if we use not those external helps to that light which God gives, to the spiritualising of our minds, we can never truly understand the things of the Spirit. Whereas, doing this, we shall be able to judge (or to discern them) clearly.

And this is that which our great master teaches us in John 7:17 where he shows us what we must do to attain a true and saving knowledge of his doctrine, *'if any man will do his will, he shall know of my doctrine, whether it be of God, or whether I speak of myself.'* And in another place, to encourage us to the practical use of what we know, he tells us, *'He that keeps my commandments, he it is that loves me, and he that loves me, shall be loved of my Father, and I will love him and manifest myself unto him'* (John 14:21). Thus have I shown you how you must endeavour to improve yourself in the knowledge of God. I now proceed to give you some further advice.

5

==

TO LIVE AS IN GOD'S SIGHT

5.1 *Containing a fifth advice, to live always as in God's sight with the great usefulness of this, to promote a holy life.*

5.2 *Containing some directions for the practice of this duty of living always as in God's sight.*

5.1 LIVE ALWAYS AS IN GOD'S SIGHT

OU MUST LIVE ALWAYS AS IN GOD'S SIGHT, or (as the words of the Psalmist are in Psalm 16:8) *'You must set God always before you'*. This is a rule of so great use in a holy life that some spiritual guides have thought that it may serve instead of all other rules. And truly, if we suppose some people to have that sound knowledge of God, which I have just now advised you to seek after, I know no reason why this one rule may not suffice. However, the usefulness of it must be acknowledged to be great, and it lies so plain, that many words need not be used to show it to you. For clear and sound apprehensions of God's majesty, of his sovereign power, unsearchable wisdom, goodness and truth will possess our hearts with love and fear, and bow our wills to his obedience, as I have shown you that they will. And surely that which will keep those apprehensions always present and in force upon our minds (as the practice of this rule will do) will keep us always resigned and obedient to him. We know by experience that the eyes of those whom we honour, and in whose favour we desire to be, have a great influence upon us and make us take heed to ourselves and to all our behaviour. Therefore, the masters of virtue among the heathens were wont to advise their scholars to imagine some excellent person, for whom they had a great veneration, to be always present with them as an observer of their actions.

And can the remembrance of God's all-seeing eye be less powerful with us, to make us circumspect in our ways and careful to approve ourselves in all things to him? Can we have a greater regard to the eyes of mortal men, whose favour or good opinion can never stand us but in little stead, than we have to the eyes of the everlasting God, in whose favour is life and in whose approbation consists our everlasting happiness? No; it is impossible. *'I have thought on your name,'* says the Psalmist, *'and have kept your law.'*

And in another place, *'my ways are always before you, therefore have I kept your precepts and your testimonies'* (Psalm 119:168). It is not unknown that some of the worst of men are sometimes restrained from doing evil by the thoughts of God's presence. And the great care that most of them take to avoid thinking upon God is no inconsiderable argument that the bearing him always in their minds would prove an absolute cure to their wickedness. For why do they put away the thoughts of him as much as they can, except because they realise that those thoughts would constrain them to become new men, and to relinquish those filthy practices which they cannot find in their hearts to forsake? It is a good story, and may fitly have a place here which we have from one of the fathers of the Church, if my memory fails me not,

Of a young man who being tempted by a wanton strumpet, seemed to consent to her unlawful desires, but required some secret place to content her. She therefore led him into a private room, and when he excepted against it as not private enough, she led him into another, and that not pleasing him, she brought him into the most secret place in the house, and told him that it was not possible any eye should see him there, or that any should come to interrupt them. But then the young man putting on a more serious countenance, demanded of her whether she thought that they could there be concealed from the eyes of almighty God? With which question, and some short discourse that was pertinent to it, he did not only cool her lust for the present, but converted her altogether from her filthy course of life.

Now, if the consideration of God's presence does sometimes work these good effects upon some of the worst of men, who neither know him truly nor love him heartily, and who have been so far from both that they have preferred the poorest objects of their lusts before him, how happy will the effects of it be upon those who have so known and loved him as to renounce both themselves and the world for his sake – who love him as much for his goodness as they fear him for his power? And who would rather die than displease him, not so much because he can punish, as because they know him to be worthy of all the love, service and obedience that they can possibly pay unto him? Surely, as those men cannot do anything but delight to think of him, they cannot help but account themselves happy that they are always under so good an eye. So the remembrance and consideration of it must needs keep them constantly resigned to him, and in all things obedient to his will. Thus much for the reason of my advice I proceed...

5.2 PRACTISE LIVING IN GOD'S SIGHT

To direct you in the practice of it. It must be confessed that it will be a hard matter for some to practise it. Those that are slaves to their flesh and to the world, and are not at liberty to think seriously of anything else, and whose consciences are burdened with the guilt of many sins, will find it very difficult, if not impossible, though they be ever so well directed. Such men must first practise the duties of self-denial and resignation. But to those that are rescued from under the tyranny of those cruel masters, and are entirely resigned to God and united to him by love, as I hope you are, nothing can be more easy, pleasant and delightful. Our souls willingly employ their thoughts upon that which they love, and gladly embrace all opportunities of being in its presence. And therefore very brief directions may suffice you concerning it, so ...

5.2.1 GOD'S OMNIPRESENCE AND OMNISCIENCE

Let me inform you that the practice of it must be grounded upon a firm persuasion of God's omnipresence and omniscience. He *'fills heaven and earth'*, as he himself tells us (Jeremiah 23:24). He encompasses them without and he fills them within. As the author to the Hebrews assures us, all things are naked and open to his eyes (4:13). They pierce to the very marrow of our bones and to the bottom of our entrails. They accompany all the extravagant wanderings of our imaginations and discover the hidden images of our memories. They look through the closet-foldings of our hearts and discern the most subtle devices of our spirits. Now, the firm belief of those things being laid for a foundation, you must accustom yourself...

5.2.2 BEHOLD GOD IN EVERYTHING

To behold God in everything. Though he is nowhere to be seen by the eye, yet your mind may perceive him in every place and in every thing, in the heavens above and in the earth beneath,

*Though he is nowhere to be seen by the eye, yet
your mind may perceive him in every place
and in every thing, in the heavens above and in
the earth beneath.*

and in every part and corner of them. In the people you converse with and in the beasts you rule over, in the fowls of the air and the fish of the sea, in the grass of the field and the trees of the forest. In yourself, and in everything round about you. In all these he may be clearly discerned exerting that power, wisdom and goodness, which first gave being to them, in sustaining, preserving and directing them. And does he thus lie open to you in everything, and has he made you capable of discerning him – and will you take no notice of him? Far be it from you. But then,

5.2.3 BEHOLD HIM IN EVERYTHING LOOKING UPON YOU

You must not only behold God in everything, but you must behold him in everything looking upon you, observing what regard you have to him, what respect you bear him, and how you demean yourself before him. As your heart must tell you that wherever you are, and whatever you look upon, that God is there, so it must tell you likewise, that there God sees you. God is with you everywhere, and his eyes are always upon you. Be also at all times with God, by an actual remembrance of him and the application of your mind unto him.

The people of Israel committed great wickedness because they said in their hearts, *'God has forsaken the earth, and the Lord sees not'* (Ezekiel 9:9). Bring your heart to tell you the contrary in all your ways, and that will restrain you from everything. But then to make this practice both more profitable and more pleasant to you, you will do well in the last place,

5.2.4 OFFER ACTS OF LOVE TO HIM

To accustom yourself to frame some acts of love upon every apprehension of God's presence, and in all humility of soul to offer them unto him. As God is worthy of the greatest love of our souls, so in everything we look upon, he appears to be so. And therefore it is very fit that we should express ourselves to be sensible of it, by some acts of love, as often as anything presents him to our minds. Now these acts may be made several ways. I will set you down some of the most chief of them, to the end that you may more readily lay hold upon all occasions that are offered you for so good an exercise. Thus,

5.2.4.1 OFFER ADMIRATION AND TRANSPORT

Thus, O God, how great is your majesty! How great is your goodness towards the sons of men! What manner of love is that wherewith you have loved us! *'O the depths of the riches, both of the wisdom and knowledge of God! How unsearchable are his judgements, and his ways past finding out!'* said St Paul (Romans 11:33).

5.2.4.2 GIVE YOUR ESTEEM AND PREFERENCE

Thus may you say, as a devout man was wont, *'My God and all things!'* And as another, *'None but Christ, None but Christ.'* And as the Psalmist, *'Whom have I in heaven but you? And there is none upon earth that I desire besides you'* (Psalm 73:25), and again, there are many that say, *'Who will show us any good? But Lord, lift up the light of your countenance upon us'* (Psalm 4:6).

5.2.4.3 OFFER PROTESTATION AND RESOLUTION

Thus St Peter thrice to his dear Lord and master, *'Lord you know that I love you'* (John 21:15). Thus the Psalmist, *'I will love you O Lord my strength'* (Psalm 18:1). And in another psalm, *'I have sworn, and I will perform it, that I will keep your righteous judgements'* (Psalm 119:106).

5.2.4.4 OFFER UP YOUR DESIRE AND ASPIRATION

Thus may you say with a holy father, *'Let me find you, O love of my soul! Let me hold you fast forever in the very midst of my heart, O blessed Life! O sovereign sweetness of my soul!'* (St Augustine). Or with the Psalmist, *'As the deer pants after the water brooks, so pants my soul after you, O God. My soul thirsts for God, for the living God, when shall I come and appear before God?'* (Psalm 42:1-2). When will the Lord call home his banished? When shall I return to my Father's house?

5.2.4.5 RESIGN YOURSELF TO GOD

As thus, 'Lord, I am yours, I am yours by a thousand titles, and I will be yours, and none but yours forever; yours I am, yours is all I have, and therefore to you do I resign myself and all.'

5.2.4.6 GIVE YOURSELF IN HUMILITY

Thus good Jacob, *'I am not worthy of the least of all your mercies'* (Genesis 32:10). And thus holy Job, *'Behold I am vile'* (Job 40:4). And thus likewise the Psalmist, *'Lord what is man, that you take knowledge of him, or the son of man, that makes account of him? Man is like to vanity, his days are as a shadow that passes away'* (Psalm 144:3-4). What are you O Lord? And what am I? Surely you are the fullness of being, but I am nothing.

5.2.4.7 RELY UPON GOD IN ALL CONFIDENCE

Can a woman forget her sucking child, that she should not have compassion on the son of her womb? Yes, she may forget, but God will not forget his people. Though my father and mother forsake me, yet the Lord will take me up. Though I perish, yet will I trust in him. He clothes the lilies of the field and feeds the fowls of the air, and will he not feed and clothe me? He has given me his only begotten son, and will he not with him give me all things?

5.2.4.8 BLESS AND PRAISE THE LORD

Thus, great is the Lord, and worthy to be praised. Yes, his name is exalted above all blessing and praise. All your works shall praise you, O Lord, and all your saints shall bless you. While I live, I will praise the Lord. I will sing praises unto God while I have any being.

These are some of the ways wherein holy men have been wont to express and exercise their love to God, and in some or other of these I would have you to be continually exercising and expressing your love according as occasion is given you, or as the things that bring God to your mind direct and lead you. You will not be long accustomed to these practices, but you will be sensible of such advantage by them, as no words of man can express. You will perceive your heart to be more closely united to God every day, and will have such a sense of his love continually upon your soul, as will make all the changes of your life comfortable, and fill you oftentimes with joy that can be compared to none but those of the saints in heaven. The truth is, we are never more like to those blessed spirits than when we are thus employed. For what do they do but contemplate the beauty of his majesty, and make acts of love to him? But here's the difference: they see him clearly as he is. They behold his unveiled face, and consequently exercise their love with the greatest fervour, and partake of the highest joys. Whereas we, beholding him only in the glass of his creatures, are much more cold in our love, and therefore less happy in our joys.

I can foresee but one thing that you can object against these exercises, namely, that they will be a hindrance to your worldly business. For this, one word may serve to remove your concern. For these being works of the soul, which is an active and most nimble substance, and not requiring the help of any member of the body, may be intermixed with all the ordinary employments. And if there be any of such a nature as will not admit them without some little stop, requiring a full application of your mind, yet that stop will be no hindrance, but rather a mighty furtherance to them. For while you do thus look up to God upon whom the success of everything depends, you will be able to proceed more cheerfully in your employments, and with greater vigour, through the confidence of his blessing upon all that you are doing.

But there is one advice more, which shall conclude this part, and may supply all that is wanting in it.

CHAPTER
6

SPIRITUAL GUIDES

CONTAINING THE LAST GENERAL ADVICE, TO COMMIT OUR
SOULS TO THE CARE AND CONDUCT OF SPIRITUAL GUIDES
WITH PROPER DIRECTIONS RELATING TO IT.

OU MUST COMMIT YOUR SOUL to the care and conduct
of a spiritual guide. For the enforcing of this advice
much might be said, and indeed, the little account
that most men make of their spiritual guides in this
age requires that much be said. But because I have set myself
but short bounds, and because I hope that you are well disposed
by the foregoing discourses to receive good counsel, I shall be
as brief as I can with respect to your good. There are three or
four things which are well known to Christians, and I hope they
will be readily acknowledged by you for great truths, which
being well considered by you, will let you know both how necessary and how beneficial this advice will be to you.

6.1 CHRIST HAS CHOSEN AN ORDER OF MINISTERS

You will acknowledge that Christ has settled an order of ministers, as his substitutes upon earth, to take care of souls to the
end of the world. This we find him doing immediately before
his ascension into heaven. Thus we read in St Matthew's Gospel
chapter 21:18,19,20 – *'All power is given unto me in heaven and in*

earth, go therefore and teach (or disciple) all nations, baptising them in the name of the Father, and of the Son, and of the Holy Ghost, teaching them to observe whatsoever I have commanded you, and lo I am with you always, even to the end of the world.' And thus we read in the sixteenth chapter of St Mark verses 15,16 – *'Go ye into all the world and preach the gospel to every creature. He that believes and is baptised shall be saved, but he that believes not shall be damned.'* And thus in the twentieth chapter of St John's Gospel, verses 21,22,23 – *As my Father has sent me, so send I you. And when he had said this, he breathed on them, and said, "receive ye the Holy Ghost. Whosoever sins ye remit, they are remitted unto them, and whosoever sins ye retain, they are retained."'* Our blessed Saviour said all this to his disciples, and no Christian can doubt and that by these words he did commit power and authority to them, which he had received from his Father for the good of men's souls. If any question be made whether this concerned the apostles only, and was confined by him only to their own persons, it may clearly be resolved by considering,

1. The importance of those words, *'I am with you always even to the end of the world'*; for how could he be with them to the end of the world, if we suppose those words to concern their persons only? They might be with him indeed, but he could not be with them to the end of the world, who were not to be in the world to the end of it, nor could they exercise the authority given them to the end of it.

2. What an unhappy condition would they be in, who were to live in succeeding ages, if no provision were made for their instruction in the Christian faith, and so forth.

3. Consider that the apostles, after they had received the Holy Ghost in an eminent and remarkable manner, according to Christ's promise, understood the commission otherwise. Therefore we find that they did by prayer and imposition of hands (the ordinary way of concerning offices among the Jews),

confer the like power upon others – as they saw good for the edification of the Church. And those persons upon whom they conferred this power are charged by them to take heed to the flock, and to feed the Church of Christ, and are said to be called and appointed thereunto by the Holy Ghost (Acts 20:28). And further, those persons that were thus ordained by the apostles are charged by them to ordain others in the same way, and directions are given them what manner of persons they were to ordain to so great an office. Thus the apostle St Paul, having put Timothy in mind of that sacred office to which he had been ordained by imposition of hands (Timothy 1:6), and of that form of sound words which he had heard from him in faith and love (v. 13), charges him *'to commit the same to faithful men, who might be able to teach others also'* (2 Timothy 2:2).

And the same apostle tells Titus, to whose care he had committed the whole Church of the Island of Crete, that he had left him there and appointed him to ordain elders, i.e. bishops and presbyters in every city (Titus 1:5). To these St Paul gives directions, *'how they should behave themselves in the Church of God'* (1 Timothy 3:15). Not only as to the ordaining of others, but likewise in many other things relating to the edification of the Church, namely,

1. As to preaching, that they should hold fast that form of doctrine which they had received, and teach that, and none other (1 Timothy 6:14, and 2 Timothy 3:14).

2. As to the public worship and service of God (1 Timothy 2:1-3). As to the holding of ecclesiastical courts, the receiving of accusations, the summoning of the accused publicly, the correcting of heretical and other disorderly persons, the stopping of their mouths, and the excommunicating of them or casting them out of the Church, charging them to prejudge no man's cause, and to do nothing for favour or partiality (1 Timothy 5:19-21; Titus 1:2; 3:10).

And so likewise as to the reconciling of penitents, and restoring them into the communion of the Church, and the hopes of pardon (1 Timothy 5:22). By all which it appears plainly that Christ did not commit the care of those souls, which he had redeemed with his most precious blood, to those only who were in a particular manner called his apostles, but that he did settle an order of ministers, and give authority to that order in a perpetual succession, to watch over them and to see that none of them perish or fall short of that happiness which he designed for them.

6.2 SPIRITUAL GUIDES ARE AUTHORISED BY CHRIST

You must acknowledge likewise that this order of ministers, thus settled by Christ to take care of souls, are authorised and empowered by him

To preach the gospel.

To make known the love of God, as manifested in Christ to the world.

To receive those that do believe the gospel into the covenant of grace, and society of Christians, by baptism.

To instruct those whom they have baptised in the will of God, both publicly and privately.

To encourage them in their obedience to it.

To excite and quicken them when they are dull and slothful.

To reprove and admonish them when they do amiss.

To restore them when they have fallen.

To comfort them in their sorrows.

To pardon their sins.

To feed them with the body and blood of Christ.

To pray for them, and bless them in Christ's name.

To help them all the ways they can in the whole course of their lives.

And to assist them in their last agonies, that so they may finish their course with joy.

This you will plainly see if you will consider, besides the places of Scripture already mentioned, the following texts, Acts 20:20,21,26,27,31; 2 Timothy 4:1,2; Galatians 6:1; Luke 22:19,20; 1 Corinthians 11:23,24; James 5:14,15.

6.3 CHRIST WILL ASSIST THE ORDER OF MINISTERS

You must acknowledge that Christ has promised to be with those his officers, and ministers, and accordingly he has, is and will be with them in the exercise of the several parts of their office to the end of the world, i.e. he will assist them with special illumination, direction and power, sufficient for the dispensation of the gospel, and the edification of the Church, and according to the necessities and capacities of the times wherein they are to live. He will furnish them with all necessary and requisite gifts, will accompany their endeavours with his Holy Spirit, to make them effectual, will hear their prayers, confirm their censures, protect their persons, etcetera.

This we are plainly taught in several places of Scripture, besides those already pointed to. See John 14:16 and 26, where Christ promises his apostles *'a Comforter to be with them for ever, and to teach them all things'*. And see Ephesians 4:11-12, where the apostle, speaking of the several offices that Christ has appointed in his Church, and of the gifts and graces which he does furnish them with, does intimate that these shall be continued in the church, in such a manner and measure as is necessary, *'till we all come* (that is, both Jews and Gentiles) *into the unity of the faith, and unto a perfect man, unto the measure of the stature of the fullness of Christ'*, i.e. to such perfection in knowledge, wisdom and goodness as that there will be no further danger of being like children tossed to and fro and carried about with every wind of doctrine (Ephesians 4:13-14).

And further, you may observe that *'as they are called the ambassadors of Christ, and are said to beseech men in Christ's stead'* (2 Corinthians 5:20), so Christ is said to speak in them and by them (2 Corinthians 13:3; Ephesians 2:17). And to work mightily and effectually in them (Galatians 2:8). And further they are said to be workers together with Christ (2 Corinthians 6:1). And to be labourers together with God (1 Corinthians 3:9). God giving the increase, while Paul planted and Apollos watered (1 Corinthians 3:6-7), and God opening men's hearts (Acts 16:14), which are said to be pricked by the apostle's preaching (Acts 2:37). Lastly, see Revelations 1:13,16, where to denote Christ's perpetual presence, assistance and protection to these his ministers or officers, the appointed guides and governors of the Church, after all the times of the apostles (John only excepted), Christ is represented though in glory, yet walking in the midst of the seven Churches of Asia, and holding the seven stars, i.e. the angels or bishops of those churches (Revelations 1:20) in his right hand.

6.4 Spiritual guides answer to Christ

You must acknowledge likewise that as Christ has appointed an order of ministers thus to guide and govern his Church, and has charged them to attend unto it with all their might, upon pain of answering for those souls that shall perish through their neglect or default (see Ezekiel 34:8-10, and Acts 20:26-27), so he has charged all men to respect them as his officers, as the guides and governors of their souls on earth under him, and to

*He will furnish them with all necessary
and requisite gifts, will accompany their
endeavours with his Holy Spirit.*

submit themselves to their conduct and government, in all things relating to the salvation of their souls. And this upon pain of losing all the privileges, advantages and benefits which they can hope for upon the account of what he has done and suffered for us.

Of this you will see no reason to doubt, if you will consider that this gracious provision which Christ has made for our souls in appointing these guides and governors, and promising them all necessary assistance for the discharge of their office, will mean very little if we may be saved while refusing to submit to them. But besides this (to give you all the satisfaction that may be in a matter which many are very unwilling to understand), you may consider some few places of Scripture which do plainly inform us of the mind of Christ concerning it. [I omit what may be said out of the Old Testament, and from the priestly power and office under it (as I have done all along), because I design not a full discourse upon those things.] As God the Father was pleased to declare,

That he had constituted his son Christ Jesus to be the supreme guide and governor of souls, and to charge all men to hear and obey him, of which we have clear testimony in Matthew 3:17 and Matthew 17:5. So Christ has left to the world a clear testimony that he did commit the authority which he had received from his Father to his apostles and their successors. (John 20:21, *'As my Father sent me, so send I you'*). And that it is his will that all must hear and obey them who will have any interest in him in order to benefit by him. In Matthew 28:19-20 and Mark 16:16, giving commission to his apostles to preach the gospel to all nations, and to receive those that should believe into that covenant of grace, which he had sealed with his blood, by baptism, he tells them: *'He that believes and is baptised shall be saved, but he that believes not, shall be damned.'* That is, those that heartily believe that gospel, which you preach and profess to do, and who engage themselves to be my disciples, and to obey my commands by receiving baptism at your hands, and who continue to learn from you what I have commanded [compare these words with those in St Matthew], and practise accordingly in the whole course of their lives, shall be saved. But those that refuse to do this shall be damned.

If we join those words which he spoke some time before to his disciples, when he sent them to preach the gospel to the lost sheep of Israel (Luke 10:16), we shall understand his mind more clearly. *'He that hears you, hears me, and he that despises you, despises me, and he that despises me, despises him that sent me.'* We see that where he has given that authority which he had received from his Father to these his ministers, so he does require all of us to own it and submit unto it. And he will consider the disowning, the not obeying, the rejecting and despising of them in the exercise of it, as the disowning, rejecting and despising of himself and his authority. And his Father likewise will judge it to be a rejecting and despising him, and his sovereign power and authority. But this is not all that the holy Scriptures speak concerning this matter. It was foreseen by God how little the generality of people would be convinced of these things. Therefore the Holy Spirit stirred up the blessed apostles, frequently to put others in mind of the authority of Christ's ministers, and the duty that we owe unto them.

Thus we find St Paul telling the Corinthians that they are the ambassadors of Christ, and stewards of the mysteries of God, and charging them to esteem them as such (1 Corinthians 4:1), and we find him beseeching the Thessalonians *'to know them that did labour among them, and were over them in the Lord, and did admonish them to esteem them very highly in love for their work's sake'* (1 Thessalonians 5:12-13). And the author to the Hebrews charges them, *'to obey them that had the rule over them* (or their guides or leaders, so the word signifies) *and to submit themselves'*.

And he backs his charge with this reason, *'that they did watch for their souls, as those that were to give account'*, i.e. they are appointed by Christ to watch for the people's souls, and they must give account to him of the souls committed to their charge. And this they can never be able to do with any comfort, if they will not obey and submit themselves to them. And making their account sad and grievous by their non-submission would be unprofitable for them. He means more than his words express, according to a way of speaking very usual in the Scriptures, i.e. this will be so far from being profitable for them that it will bring the greatest damage and mischief to them, namely, the ruin and perdition of their souls.

I forbear to mention any more places of Scripture, and I omit to urge the practice of the first and best Christians, as also the sinful characters that are given by some of the holy writers, of those that did slight the guides and governors of the Church, and refuse to submit themselves unto them, because I have promised not to be tedious.

Now having carefully observed and seriously weighed these things, give me leave to put some few questions briefly to you. Do you believe that there is no need of these spiritual guides in the world? If there is no need of them, why did Christ appoint them? Why did he not leave people to themselves in the concerns of their souls, as he has done in those things that concern their bodies and their outward estates? Was there need of guides for the first preaching of Christianity to the world, and is there no need of them for the propagation and maintenance of it in the world? I forbear to remind you of the natural blindness of people's understandings, with the inconsiderateness, rashness, levity, inconstancy, which is inseparable to human nature.

We may be confident that if Christ had not known that the world needed spiritual guides, he would never have appointed any such, nor have promised them their assistance, which you have now heard of, nor have taken any care to inform us of the duty we do owe unto them. And therefore are not those people too much pushed up in their fleshly minds, or too regardless of the everlasting interests, that account these guides to be of no use to them, or are wanting in that respect for them and dependence upon them which they ought to have? I doubt not but you will admit it. But further, do you not understand by what has been said, that we may receive very great advantages from our spiritual guides if we accept them? Surely, those of old that received them as the Galatians did (4:14), as the angels of God, yes, even as Christ Jesus, did believe so. Besides, was not the making of this provision for the good of men's souls a great demonstration of Christ's love and care for them?

And therefore must not they be great despisers of the love of Christ and enemies of their own souls that make little account of it and seek no advantage by it? Or can they with the least shadow of reason call themselves Christians, or expect to be partakers of those benefits which he has promised to his faithful servants, who have no regard at all to his ordinances and institutions, or no other regard to them than as they please their own dispositions and are agreeable to their stubborn wills? I doubt not but you will answer to these demands according to my heart's desire, and therefore you cannot but acknowledge that my advice is good and useful.

Commit your soul to the care and conduct of a spiritual guide. I proceed now to show you briefly how you must practise this advice.

*Your soul is a jewel of too great a value
to be put into the hands of every pretender,
yes, or of every one whose office it is to
take care of souls.*

CHAPTER
7
==

THE PRACTICE OF THE FORMER ADVICE

OU MUST MAKE A CHOICE of a good guide. I call him a good guide, who having authority from Christ, is able to direct you aright in all the concerns of your soul and will be faithful to you. Christ has nowhere promised that none shall take upon them to be guides of souls, but those that have authority from him. Nor has he promised that all those that have authority from him shall discharge their office faithfully. Among his twelve apostles there was a Judas, and among the seven deacons ordained by the apostles, tradition tells us, there was one that failed. And in those writings that we have of some of the apostles, we find complaints of some that loved the world more than Christ, and their own fleshly lusts more than the good of souls. And St Peter has told us that 'as there were of old false prophets among God's people, so there shall be false teachers among Christians, who through covetousness shall with feigned words make merchandise of them' (2 Peter 2:1,2,3).

And therefore it is no matter of wonder if there be some such among us now, but it ought to be matter of caution to you, to whom you do trust your soul. Your soul is a jewel of too great a value to be put into the hands of every pretender, yes, or of every one whose office it is to take care of souls. And those that are ready to follow the conduct and counsel of every one that will take upon him to be their guide or instructor, are not much less to be blamed than those that will commit their souls to none. And therefore, you are to take the greatest care, and to use the best skill you have in the choice of your guide. And because it is a matter of no little difficulty to make a right choice, it will not, I hope, be thought impertinent to give you some assistance.

7.1 PRAY IN PRIVATE FOR GOD'S HELP

I advise you to go to your closet, and to beg of God to direct you in your choice. Even if you have ever so much skill in judging of men, yet it is possible that in this case you may be deceived. And the more you trust to your own skill, the greater danger you are in of being deceived, God usually suffering those that have a great opinion of themselves to miscarry in their best undertakings. Therefore in this, as well as in other things, your security lies in an humble confidence in God's direction, which you are to beg of him by fervent prayer. Though the blessing be great, yet you have no reason to doubt but that you shall obtain it, if you do ask it aright. For since he has done so much for your soul already, he will not deny you anything. You may be confident that he knows what is necessary for its welfare and happiness. *'If any of you lack wisdom, let him ask of God, who gives to all men liberally, and upbraids not, and it shall be given him'* (James 1:5). And what greater wisdom can you desire than that which may enable you to choose a good guide, except it be that which may enable you to follow him, when you have made choice of him? Which you are also to ask of God. But then,

7.2 Use the skill God gives you in choosing a guide

Though you must not confide in your own skill, but in the assistance and direction of almighty God, yet, since his assistance and direction can be expected only in a rational way, it will behoove you to make use of that skill which God gives you, and that, with as much care as if your success depended altogether upon it. This, in other matters, you think yourself bound to, and I can see no reason why you should not be of the same mind in this case. You must therefore look out into the world, and consider who among those guides of souls that are known to you is most fit to be trusted. And if you do desire the opinion of some serious and discreet friends, as you are wont to do when you need a physician for your body, or a lawyer for settling your estate, I think you will do very well. Only let me caution you that you do not presume to make judgement of any one with whom you are not thoroughly acquainted, for otherwise – though it is possible you may hit right – yet it is two to one that you will be deceived, which will be a fault that will admit of no excuse.

And the same caution you are to take in receiving the judgements of others. Consider that as some people have a better repute in the world than they do deserve, so others have a worse. And it is commonly observed that many excellent men have suffered very much, merely because others have given credit to the reports of those who were never intimately acquainted with them, and yet have presumed to pass their censures on them. But to help you as much as I can in this matter, which is really of very great importance to you, it will not be amiss to give you a short account of the qualifications and properties of a good guide, referring you for further instruction to the epistles of St Paul to Timothy and Titus. And

7.2.1 A GOOD GUIDE IS ONE THAT HAS RECEIVED AUTHORITY FROM CHRIST TO TAKE CARE OF SOULS

If it be true that none can give that which they have not to give, and none can be presumed to have received that which was never given to them, you then have great reason to believe that some persons, who pretend to ministry, have no authority from Christ to take care of souls.

You may perhaps hear them speak many good things of themselves and their followers, and make great boast of the Spirit of Christ, but when you have impartially considered the heresies, schisms, seditions, tumults, rebellions, murders, rapines, perjuries, which they have been the authors and promoters of, you will know how to judge of their great boasts and godly pretensions.

By these their fruits you may know them. I say no more, nor indeed should I have said so much, but that the disorders of the age do make it necessary to give them some little caution.

7.2.2 A GOOD GUIDE IS A PERSON OF KNOWLEDGE

He is able to teach you as much as you are bound to believe and practise. His lips preserve knowledge and his tongue can show you right things. He cannot be a good guide to others who has need of a guide himself. *'If the blind lead the blind, both will fall into the ditch'* (Matthew 15:14).

7.2.3 HE IS A MAN OF PRUDENCE AND DISCRETION

Which appears both by his conversation, and in the exercise of his ministry, fitting his instructions to the necessities and capacities of his people. *'He pours not new wine into old bottles.'* He feeds not children with strong meat, and strong men with milk. He provides for every one what is fitting for him, and that in due season. Indiscretion does oftentimes as much mischief as the grossest ignorance.

7.2.4 HE IS HUMBLE, MEEK AND PEACEABLE

So was the great shepherd and bishop of our souls. He was no lordly, domineering person, no breaker of the peace of the world, or overturner of governments, but was a servant unto all, even to the meanest of the people. He pleased not himself, but others for their good, and submitted himself patiently and quietly to the authority of the chief priests and of the Roman emperor.

7.2.5 HE HAS A SENSE OF SACREDNESS OF HIS OFFICE

He is very grave and serious not out of sourness or sullenness or humour, but from a real sense of the sacredness of his office, the worth of souls, and the account he must give of them. It is said of a devout man that when some desired him to give them a certain mark by which they might know a man to be truly spiritual, he answered them in this manner, 'If ye see anyone that takes delight in the common sportings, and jestings, the railleries and drolleries of the world, that cannot patiently suffer contempt and reproach, take heed that you believe not that man to be spiritual, though you should see him work miracles.'

This good man was undoubtedly in the right, and I think he had not been mistaken if he had omitted the latter part concerning the not suffering contempt, and given the affectation of wit and drollery for a sufficient mark of a very imperfect Christian. However, it may serve for a mark to discover a bad guide. For if every Christian should be a serious person (because Christ was so), the ambassadors of Christ should be much more so. Their deportment should be such as may awe the men they do converse with, and in a silent way deter them from their sins. And their persons should speak what the statue of Senacherib is said to have done, *'He who looks to me, let him be religious.'* But though a good guide be thus grave and serious, yet he is not crabbed, morose or cynical; but,

7.2.6 HE CAN CARRY ON AFFABLE CONVERSATION

An affable and courteous and sweet and winning conversation. He disdains not to converse with the meanest people, and that freely and cheerfully too, nor to conform himself to all the innocent customs of the world, so far as consists with the sacredness of his office and the decorum of his person. Having a due respect to those, he becomes all things to all people, and though his gravity shows him to be an enemy to their sins, yet his innocent and cheerful compliances show him to be a lover of their persons. There was never any person more remarkable for this than our blessed Saviour, who though his gravity was such that he was never seen to laugh, as we know of, yet was he of so sweet and benign a temper, and so courteous and compliant in all his carriage and conversation, that none were ever offended at it. To his example does every good guide of souls conform himself in this as well as in other things.

7.2.7 He is a Man of Courage

He fears not the faces of the greatest persons upon earth, nor is discouraged in the doing of his duty by the thoughts of their displeasure. He is another John the Baptist in this respect, who was not afraid to tell the tyrant Herod that it was not lawful for him to have his brother's wife (Mark 16:18). And like St Paul, he can be contented if God will have it so, *'not only to be bound, but to die for the name of the Lord Jesus'* (Acts 21:13).

7.2.8 He is Wholly Devoted to the Work that Christ has Appointed him to Do

It is his only business and sole care, and as Christ said of himself, that it was his meat and drink to do the will of his Father, so 'tis his to do the will of Christ, in taking care for souls. He is no plodder for the world, no seeker of the fleece, no hunter after preferment. These worldly things are as dross and dung to him, and he will not sell poor souls for such gains.

7.2.9 He is a Great Lover of Souls

And of much tenderness and compassion towards them, he will do anything, yes, suffer any thing for their good, and lay down his life (if need be) for their sakes. He is grieved for their miscarriages more than for all worldly things, *'as Christ was grieved for the hardness of men's hearts'*, and is better pleased with their well doing, than by the greatest earthly prosperity. They are his joy and crown that do well by his ministry. He thinks no honour greater, and knows no greater joy.

Lastly, he is a man of a holy life. His example teaches us as much as his tongue, and he is a pattern for his people to walk by. His conversation is in heaven, and he can boldly call upon others to be followers of him, and to walk as they have him for an example. Though he is not without his failings and imperfections, as he is flesh and blood, yet no crimes or gross sins, nor any indulging or allowing of himself in the least, can the sharpest and most malicious eye behold in him.

Thus have I given you a short account of the qualifications of a good guide. Such a guide you may boldly commit your soul to, and if you will follow his discretions, he will keep you through the grace of God from all things hurtful, and lead you into all things profitable for your salvation.

7.2.9.1 ACCEPT A QUALIFIED PASTOR IN YOUR PARISH

But there is one thing that I am concerned in this place to mind you of, namely that if the pastor of the parish wherein you live be thus qualified, you have a guide provided for you, and you must seek no further, for he has the charge of your soul committed to him by God, and he must give an account of it to God. Besides, you cannot reasonably expect the blessing of God under the conduct of another if, to please yourself, you do act clean contrary to the ordinance of God, and prefer your own wisdom before the wisdom of his providence. You cannot hope to fall under the conduct of a good guide if you do reject him who by the appointment of God ought to have the conduct of you. No honest and prudent guide will allow of this practice, or take the care of any upon him that belong to another parish except it be when that church is so under the conduct of one that is either grossly ignorant or notoriously vicious. What I have said therefore of looking out for a guide you must understand as meant only when the church to which you do belong is in this unhappy condition. In this case you are to follow the directions before given, but in no other. But to proceed,

7.2.9.2 ASK HIM TO TAKE YOU INTO HIS CARE

Being resolved as to the person you design for your guide, I advise you to go to him and inform him of your desire to save your soul. Put yourself under his conduct in order to beseech him to receive you into his care, and to give you such directions as he shall think necessary and fitting for you, assuring him that you will follow them to the utmost of your power. Endeavour to show yourself a good Christian in submitting yourself to him, as to Christ's minister, and by depending altogether upon him. And that he may be the better judge of the honesty and sincerity of your heart in what you tell him, and know what directions you have most need of, do not be ashamed to make yourself fully known to him. Tell him what manner of education you have had, what manner of life you have led, what convictions you have had at any time of the evil of sin, what resolutions you have taken upon those convictions, how far you have made them good, and wherein you have failed. Acquaint him with your natural temper, and your acquired inclinations. Tell him what evil habits you have contracted, what vicious customs you have been or are engaged in, what temptations you have found yourself most inclined to, and overcome by, and so forth.

In a word, I advise you to open your very soul unto him (he will help you to do it by seasonable and fitting questions, if he finds you willing) and conceal not the least thing from him.

You would not scruple to discover the state of your body to your physician when you need his help. Why then should you be shy of acquainting your spiritual physician with the state of your soul? Are you more ashamed of the diseases of your soul than you are of the infirmity of your body? The greater reason you have to desire their cure, and in order to it to make them known.

Will your physician keep the infirmities of your body secret? No less safe will the secrets of your soul be in the bosom of your spiritual guide. Away then with that imprudent and unreasonable modesty, which will not do you the least good, but may be the occasion of your ruin. Hear what a heathen man, Plutarch, has said in criticism of those who do not disclose their ills, and blush at the folly of those that call themselves Christians.

"You say unto a vicious man, hide yourself with your vices, endure your pestilent and dangerous disease, conceal your envy and superstition as you hide certain paintings (pornographic), and beware that you give not yourself to such as can instruct and heal you." (This is the advice of the devil and his instruments upon earth.)

The ancients exposed their sick men to open view, that such as passed by, and had been sick of the same diseases, or had given ease and help thereunto, might signify so much unto the sick man. And they affirmed that the art itself, improved by such experience, to have been much bettered thereby.

In like manner it may seem expedient to lay open the sins of our life, and the evil affections of the mind, that it may be lawful for any considering and beholding the same to say,

Are you angry? Take heed of this.

Are you in love? I myself was so, but have repented.

Now, when some men hide their vices, deny, and conceal them, what do they do but fasten them more thoroughly and surely to themselves?

Thus I do make the greater account of Plutarch's words because of those of St James, chapter 5:16 – *'Confess your faults one to another, and pray one for another.'* If we understand this as making known our sins to our Christian brethren, that they may the better understand what petitions to put up to God in our behalf, then they agree exactly with the heathen's advice – though it be grounded upon another motive. But the truth is, the words *'confess your faults therefore to one another'* plainly refer to the words before, concerning the elders of the Church, and their prayers for the sick, and the effect of those prayers.

But to let this pass, it is enough for my present purpose that it be granted to be expedient for believers, in order to advance their spiritual welfare, to confess their sins to their Christian brethren. If it be so, I think it is not to be denied that it is more expedient for them to confess to those whose office it is to pray for them, and to counsel them, and who have ministerial authority from Christ to pronounce the pardon and absolution of true penitents. But to proceed,

7.2.9.3 Listen to him as you would listen to Christ

Having thus acquainted the spiritual guide with your desires, and having fully opened yourself unto him, set yourself to receive his instructions. Hear him as you would hear Christ himself, whose minister he is, speaking to you. Mark what he says with the greatest care. If anything fall from him, which you do not fully understand, desire him to explain his meaning. If you do distrust your memory, his instructions being many, desire him to repeat them and when he has made an end, give him, together with your thanks, your promise to follow his directions. And so begging his prayers, and his blessing in the name of Christ, take your leave of him.

7.2.9.4 RECOLLECT AND PRACTISE WHAT HE ADVISES

As soon as you are gone from him, begin to recollect the good advice you have received, and to practise accordingly and omit not the doing of anything he has advised you to. If anything he has advised you to seems hard, or without reason, yet reject it not, but consider that though you do not perceive the reason why he has laid such things upon you, yet he may have seen good reason for it. You do not know but it was to try the sincerity of the profession you have made to him, and to know the better how to fit himself to your necessities hereafter. Or it may be he might (in prudence) design that you should not understand the reason of some particular advices, till you feel the good effect of them, and the great advantages they bring you, to dispose you the more readily and cheerfully to follow him for the future. For finding great benefit in that, in which you could foresee none, as well as in that which did promise you much, you cannot but think yourself happy in meeting with such a guide, so you cannot but be mightily encouraged by it, and give him the entire disposal of you for the time to come.

Be careful then to observe his directions in everything, remembering that as a sick man can receive no benefit by the best physician in the world, no matter how well he has made him understand his disease, if he puts up his prescriptions in his pocket and makes no further use of them – so the instructions of your guide (no matter how good they may be in themselves) will be of no advantage to you if you do not follow them. Indeed, let me add (which you are concerned to remember), that your case will be much worse than the case of such an imprudent person, for though he is not to be benefited by the prescriptions of his physician, yet he can receive no hurt by his not using them. Whereas you will receive much damage by neglecting those that have been given you, for besides this, all insincere dealing in matters of religion, and trifling in holy things, does in itself tend to harden the heart and to make you more regardless of the great concerns of your soul. It will certainly provoke God to withdraw his grace from you, and to leave you to fall into that ruin and destruction which you are but little afraid of and take no care to avoid.

7.2.9.5 TELL HIM WHAT YOU HAVE DONE WITH HIS INSTRUCTIONS

Return to your guide after some time, and give him an impartial account of the use you have made of his instructions, and the benefit you have received by them. If you have failed in anything, confess it freely, and declare your resolution to do better for the time to come. If you can say that you have failed in nothing, give God thanks, and say as the young man did to our blessed Saviour, Matthew 19:20, *'What lack I yet?'* And then receive his directions as you did before, and take care to practise accordingly.

7.2.9.6 KEEP A CONSTANT CORRESPONDENCE WITH HIM AS LONG AS YOU LIVE

Acquaint him from time to time with the state and condition of your soul, with your progress in wisdom and virtue, with your temptations and discouragements, with your failings and imperfections, with your doubts and fears, with your joys and sorrows, and undertake not anything of moment or importance without his advice and approbation. You will quickly be sensible of such advantages by this course which will effectually encourage you to proceed in it. You will constantly enjoy peace and satisfaction in your own mind by it, having not only the approbation of your own conscience in everything you do, but also the approbation of one of Christ's ministers, who is better able to judge of your actions – and may be presumed to judge more impartially than yourself would do.

It may suffice to mention some of those services he will be continually doing for you. He will instruct you in what you are ignorant of, and will either prevent or rectify your mistakes. He will resolve your doubts, and remove your fears, and ease you of your sorrows. He will restrain you when you are too zealous and forward, and quicken you when you are dull and slothful, and refresh and cheer you when you are aweary. He will restore you when you are fallen, and apply the promises of the gospel to you, and help you to take comfort in them. He will remove many difficulties out of your way, and arm you against temptations, and support you under trials, and be both a guide and a guardian to you in all the dangerous and troublesome passages of your life. In a word, he will make you to understand your duty fully, to know what is necessary, and what is lawful, and what is expedient, and what is seasonable. And help you to distinguish between truth and falsehood, reality and appearance, good and evil. He will excite and stir up your will to embrace the one and refuse the other. He will moderate your affections, and keep your passions in order, and preserve you in an even, steady course of well-doing, and at least deliver you up in peace and safety into the hands of the great shepherd and bishop of our souls, Christ Jesus.

Objection. But it may be you will meet with some that will ask you, what necessity is there for all this? Why may it not be enough for your salvation, which is enough for the salvation of most people, who live and die, and go to heaven without all this trouble, contenting themselves to have a minister in their parish, to hear him preach, and to receive the sacrament of communion from his hands? Without putting themselves or him to so much trouble concerning their souls. If they may be saved without all this ado, why may not you? It is not good to be private and set apart and they that teach men to be so are not their friends.

Answer. To those men, many things may be replied, but it may suffice to offer these few things to their consideration. We do not take upon us to judge of the everlasting state of any. We leave that to be manifested in that day which shall bring to light the most hidden things. We do not bind men to take this course upon pain of everlasting damnation. But surely, every man is concerned to endeavour to save his own soul, and whether the best way to do this be to do as the most do, or to do as I have advised you, do you judge. Look into your world and observe the daily miscarriages of those men whose practice you are urged to approve and imitate. How many of them after many years going to church and hearing sermons, have no more understanding in the very principles of their religion than they had when they were children? And of some we may say, as St Paul did *'that they are ever learning, but never able to come to the knowledge of the truth'* (2 Timothy 3:7).

7.2.9.7 TELL YOUR ADVISOR YOUR WEAKNESSES

How many are puffed up with a great opinion of their own knowledge, that know nothing as they ought to know, and will never know anything because those that should and would instruct them cannot know their ignorance till it is too late to give them instructions? How many of them become a prey to seducers, and drink in damnable doctrines, with as much eagerness as they should do the most saving truths, merely because they take upon them to judge of everything, and will not take advice of those whom God has set over them to direct them?

How many go groaning under the burden of troubled consciences for many years, and become desperate, and lay violent hands upon themselves, because they would not admit their grief to a spiritual physician, who might have poured wine and oil into their wounds, and have bound them up to their everlasting peace and comfort? How many go on in an evil course who might be persuaded to leave it, but for some prejudices which they have entertained either against a good life in general or some particular duties, or against some doctrine, which if received would work a reformation in them, and which prejudices Christ's ministers cannot remove, because they know them not? How many that mean well and make many good promises and resolutions, are overcome by their lusts and the temptations of the devil and the world, merely for want of particular directions as to those lusts and those temptations? These sad shipwrecks, and many more which you may daily behold, may convince you how dangerous it is to go in the common way, and how much safer it will be for you to follow the advice that I have given you. And if people will not be persuaded that it is their duty to do thus, I am sure they may see that it is so much in their interest that they cannot despise it without despising their own souls.

And as for the threat of being alone, which you may be warned about, it is but what the best of Christ's disciples have undergone in all ages, and no good Christian will make any reckoning of it. Were we to please men, we should have reason to dread it, but since our business is to please God, and to save our souls, it is no matter what they either say or think of us.

*These sad shipwrecks, and many more which you may
daily behold, may convince you how dangerous it is to go in
the common way, and how much safer it will be
for you to follow
the advice that I have given you.*

Suppose, my friend, that Christ had shown himself as much concerned for the health of our bodies, or the increase of our estates, as he has done for the salvation of our souls. That he had appointed an order of ministers to teach us how to get money, or to preserve ourselves in health and strength for many years, and had given them as strict a charge to take care of it, and be diligent in it, and had promised them as great assistance to make their cares and endeavours effectual to these ends, as he has done to the appointed guides of souls. And that he had commanded all the people as strictly to respect them as his officers appointed to these purposes, to follow their directions, and submit themselves in all things to them, as he has commanded them to submit to their spiritual guides.

Supposing this, I say, do you think that people would behave themselves in that manner towards these good friends of their bodies, as they do the great friends and guides of their souls? Would they content themselves to hear them read once or twice a week a public lecture of medicine, or good husbandry? No, no, we should see every man running to their houses and desiring private conversation with them. We should hear one saying, *'Sir, you take great pains among us, and read very well and learnedly, but I am a poor ignorant man, and understand but little, and remember less, and therefore I pray you to explain and repeat some of those good things to me, which you speak in public.'* And another we should hear complaining that he could receive no benefit by all his pains, because his discourses were not proper for his care, and therefore, would beseech him to consider his particular needs and to give him suitable directions, and so forth.

This we may well suppose people would do, from what we see them do now when they need the advice of physicians and those of skill in worldly matters. And we may boldly say that they would not spare (keeping still to the former supposition) to make loud outcries against the appointed physicians as being false to their trust if they should refuse to hear them in private, and refer them only to their public lectures. Now let any one tell me, why people do not take this same course for their souls, which they would take for their bodies and estates? Will they say that their souls have not so much need of the help of Christ's ministers as their bodies have of the help of physicians? And that they themselves know better how to secure their spiritual and eternal welfare than they do their temporal? This would betray more stupid ignorance, or devilish pride and self-conceit, than they will be willing to admit.

Will they say that the ministers may understand the particular necessities of every person, and provide for them without their taking the course prescribed, and that they may suit their public instructions, exhortations and directions to everyone's capacities, no matter how different they are?

This will be to make them more than prophets, to ascribe a kind of omniscience to them. Yes, and an omnipotence too to make their sermons, as God is said by some to have made the manna in the wilderness, agreeable to the taste of everyone – which I suppose no one in his wits will do. What then is the reason of it? For my part, I can give no other than this, that either they are grossly ignorant and little better than beasts in understanding, or mere infidels under the name of Christians. Or if they do in some sort believe the gospel, yet their hearts are so engaged to the world that they cannot have any serious and constant regard to their immortal souls.

But, to put an end to this matter, whether the cause of the common practice be good or bad, I am sure the effects of it are sad and lamentable. The great decay of Christian piety among us, the great increase of all manner of wickedness, the multiplying of errors, schisms and divisions, has no one more visible cause than this. And till people are convinced that they owe a greater respect to their spiritual guides than their practice demonstrates, and will be persuaded to follow the advice I have now given them, I cannot hope to see any stop put to these evils.

I beseech you therefore, my friend, by all that is dear to you, not to despise my counsel. Defer not to make the choice of a guide, and when you have done so, be not slack to desire his advice, nor to fail to follow it. You may be confident of the blessing of God in so doing. Your guide is particularly concerned to give you the best advice he can, and God is concerned to make it effectual for your good, since he has particularly ordained it for that end.

To these directions I might add many more, namely, that you will do well to endear yourself to your guide as much as you can, that he may take the greater care of you, and be more ardently desirous of your salvation. To which purpose you may do well to show your esteem of him by a respectful carriage before others. And further, you may do well to contribute cheerfully, according to your ability, towards his maintenance, if he be not plentifully provided for. The *primitive* Christians do not fail to do this as you may perceive by their devoting all that they had to the service of Christ and his Church (Acts 4:34-35). The sacrilege of many that call themselves Christians in this age make it necessary for good Christians to do the same now.

And you must keep close to your guide as long as you live, and never change him for another if God's providence does not constrain you.

In all your intercourse with your guide, you must look beyond him, namely, to your God, whose minister he is, and who guides and blesses you by his ministry, and for whom you must daily address yourself by prayer for a blessing upon his endeavours – and it is to God to whose goodness and mercy you must daily ascribe all the benefit you do receive by them.

But I must forbear, having too far exceeded my bounds already. I conclude all with the words of our dear Lord and Saviour, *'Now you know these things, happy are you if you do them'* (John 13:17).

The End